THE COASTAL COOK
of West Marin

100 Kitchen conversations and recipes
Illustrations by Bonita Barlow
By Laura Riley

Copies of this book may be ordered from:
The Coastal Cook
P.O. Box 925
Bolinas, CA 94924

Or the office of The Point Reyes Light:
P.O. Box 210
Point Reyes Station, CA 94956

Riley and Company
P.O. Box 925
Bolinas, CA 94924

ISBN: 0-9628426-0-5

Cover Art and Illustrations: Bonita Barlow
Cover Design: Drake Jordan
Design Consultants: Elizabeth Moralis-Denney & Cyndie C.H. Wooley
Copyediting: Tracy Thompson, Zoe Scott, Ned Riley
Computer Assistant: Bert Crews
Dark Room Work: Eric Firpo

ACKNOWLEDGEMENTS

I would like to thank the following people, for their encouragement and assistance, without whom this book would never have become a reality:

Margot Patterson Doss
Robert Mowry
Marjorie and Edward C. Riley
Ned Riley and Jennifer Pfieffer
David V. Mitchell
Tracy Thompson
Bonita Barlow
Bert Crews
Zoe Scott, Janet Gallagher, Missy Patterson,
Renée Shannon, Kerry Shipley
and the encouraging staff at
The Point Reyes Light
Eric Firpo
Marty Knapp
Drake and Helen Jordan
Michael Sykes
Cindy Ohama
Elizabeth Moralis Denney
Cyndie C.H. Wooley
Mel Fiske
Michael Rafferty, who gave me the idea
Margaret Frings Keyes

FROM THE EDITOR:

By Dave V. Mitchell,
Editor and Publisher, *The Point Reyes Light*

Whether we're reading Edwin Arlington Robinson's poems about the people of Tilbury Town or Sherwood Anderson's stories about the residents of Winesburg, Ohio, most of us find life in a small town fascinating. Because residents of small towns know their neighbors and are known by them, townspeople never become anonymous members of the herd in the way big city dwellers often do.

That is what makes Laura Riley's *The Coastal Cook* so special. As much as it is about recipes, the book is also about the residents of a dozen neighboring small towns that make up a rural area known as West Marin on the coast of Northern California.

Author Laura Riley is both a columnist and typesetter for *The Point Reyes Light,* a country weekly which covers West Marin. At a small paper such as *The Light* (circulation 3,800), most of the staff do double duty. I am both the editor and janitor; the reporters also deliver newspapers.

This cookbook is drawn from Laura Riley's weekly column, The Coastal Cook, one of *The Light's* most popular features. It is based on those columns which featured both good recipes and good stories about the cooks. The two don't always go together . One column not included profiled a TV reporter who lives in Stinson Beach. A wonderfully witty man, he has survived the vicissitudes of an insecure profession in good humor, and his story was delightful. Unfortunately, his recipe was rather minimal: Jack Daniel's On the Rocks. The recipes Laura Riley chose for this book reveal noticeably more imagination.

West Marin is not Winesburg or Tilbury Town. It's far more heterogeneous than either. But the townspeople you will meet in this book share a sense of community. They love their coast, and open fields, and nature, but above all, they know their fellow townspeople well enough to care about them.

— DVM

INTRODUCTION

There are few places of such captivating beauty as the rural half of Marin County. Many hearts are stolen on their first visit. A drive along the Marin coast on Highway 1 is usually all it takes — not during the summer months of course, when you can't see the guardrails for the fog, but rather on a clear autumn or spring day.

This seduction occurred for me 12 years ago at what I call the "Ahhh" turn on Panoramic Highway coming over Mount Tamalpais toward Stinson Beach and saw the graceful curve of the beach from a hawk's eye view.

West Marin is an abundant land. The Miwok Indians who once populated this region revelled in the land's productivity. Then, as now, Marinites lived high on the hog, enjoying the beaches, lagoons and bays rich with fish and shellfish. Today, the valleys and flatlands where wild game was once plentiful provide a good share of the organic produce consumed by Bay Area diners.

Through the vision and persistence of a few innovative and creative minds, much of this land will remain protected from development forever. The Point Reyes National Seashore, the Golden Gate National Recreation areas, the Bolinas Lagoon Nature Preserve, the Farallon Island Wildlife Refuge are live testimony of great effort put forth by people who love and respect this land.

My career as a writer began in 1985 as a reporter for the Pulitzer Prize-winning *Point Reyes Light* — as a Bolinas "stringer," which meant I covered school board meetings, water board meetings and performances, as well as doing interviews and photography of whatever made an interesting picture.

In 1987, The Light sent out a Readers' Survey, to find out what the readership wanted to see more or less of in the paper. There were a surprising number of requests for the return of *The Coastal Cook*, a feature in *The Point Reyes Light* long before me. There were, in fact, many writers of *The Coastal Cook* through the 1970s and 80s. Fred Graeser, and Jeff Probst each wrote the column for a year or two. Sometimes The Cook was a shared responsibility for the staff at The Light.

Publisher Dave Mitchell then asked if I was interested in writing it. Since I love to talk, love to eat, and found it challenging to meet new people and find out what they eat, I jumped at the chance.

At first, I was more interested in the people I met than in the recipes they gave me. Most of my interviewees were greatly amused when, after a long, sometimes philosophical discussion, I asked them for a recipe. But usually the request was just the right ingredient to bring the whole conversation down to earth. I found that the mention of food is a universal equalizer. After all, we all eat. And we all enjoy an artfully prepared meal. Even the most esoteric, undomestic individuals became endearing when they found themselves wrestling with the proportions of a recipe.

Time after time I have knocked on the doors of folks I did not yet know, with a tiny knot of apprehension in my stomach. Again and again I have been reassured that there are fascinating and generous people who are eager to tell what it is that moves them — and what they love to eat.

I never tire of people's stories. To my surprise, I grow more interested and more curious as I talk to more and more people. Sometimes I know absolutely nothing about the subject they have made their life's work. Sometimes I struggle to accurately represent their thoughts. Always I am amazed at the integrity, quality, and generosity of people in the West Marin community.

In the following pages, I invite you to meet 100 residents of West Marin, selected by chance and by choice, who begin to describe what this place is all about.

— Laura Riley

TABLE OF CONTENTS

Soups & Chowders

Breads & Muffins

TABLE OF CONTENTS

Salads & Dressings

Seafood Entrées

TABLE OF CONTENTS

Vegetarian Entrées

TABLE OF CONTENTS

Meat & Poultry

Mexican Entrées

TABLE OF CONTENTS

Sweet Things

Drinks & Whatnot

SOUPS & CHOWDERS

BILL QUIST

Concert pianist Bill Quist padded out onto his deck to greet me in shorts and tousled hair, on one sultry hot midday. We stepped inside the cool of the home he shares with Susie Stewart, on Horseshoe Hill Road where his grand piano also resides.

"I made this great gazpacho," he offered, "or we can have carrot soup, lentils with delicious sausages or just cheese sandwiches." As he dug around in the fridge, we chatted.

"The thing that really got me into music was this fabulous high school I went to called Interlochen Arts Academy. There I was in this community of artists in the woods of northern Michigan," he said. "But I started playing piano at five. My God, that means I've been playing 35 years now. Gives away my age doesn't it?" We settled on gazpacho.

"I'm not into practicing endless technique," he explained. "I think technique is solved musically." With that he leapt up to the piano to demonstrate. Rocking forward on the bench, he turned the simple notes of a major scale into pure romance. "If you always practice musically, you always will be musical." He popped back into the kitchen to serve the soup.

"For me, music is the sheer pleasure of listening to sound. It nourishes the soul and it really is *the* international language... I've been playing for Bread and Roses for about 15 years. We go into hospitals, nursing homes and psych wards and play. Since I can't afford to give money and I have lots of energy and music, I've done lots of benefits over the years."

Quist was the first pianist hired by Will Ackerman of Windham Hill Records. Ackerman heard a tape of Quist's music and asked him to record the music of Eric Satie. "I was in my early 20s then; it was really an honor with all these great masters around. I was lucky — the recording got rave reviews."

He has played with both the San Francisco Symphony and Chorus, but loves the intimacy of playing chamber music with just a few other musicians. He also sings with the professional Baroque Arts Ensemble. And he supports local musicians in composing new music by commissioning work funded by grants and enthusiastic patrons of the arts.

His ability to sight read came in handy in playing with the Chorus: "When I first started, sometimes I'd get the music for the first time at 10 a.m. the morning of the rehearsal."

Quist was the original pianist for the West Marin Community Chorus. "We came out from San Francisco to Barbara Pace's home for a dress rehearsal of a show. I stayed all day. I'd never seen anything like it — this marvelous modern woman with two Steinway grand pianos and a huge garden. I came to live with Barbara for five years.

"Barbara Pace is a great cook. I learned all about vegetables from her. This recipe has evolved over the years with a little improvisation from others," said Quist.

Broccoli Soup

Ingredients:

2 chopped onions
2 Tbsp. butter
2 bunches broccoli
8 cloves garlic
1 quart chicken broth
2 potatoes, peeled, cubed
favorite herbs (lemon thyme, sage, for example)
1 Tbsp. mustard
Dash of Worchestershire sauce

Method:

While onions sauté slowly in the butter over low to medium heat, deflower the broccoli. Put aside.

Peel the broccoli stems and boil them whole in chicken stock with garlic and herbs.

When onions are golden brown, put aside and lightly sauté broccoli flower tops, cut in small pieces.

Blend broccoli stems, garlic, stock, potatoes and mustard and Worchestershire sauce.

Add the broccoli tops and onions to the blended mixture and simmer for 15 minutes. Serve with lemon wedges and chopped parsley. When re-heating any left-over soup, add milk or cream for variety.

YVONNE RAND

An ordained priest and meditation teacher of the Soto-Zen Buddhist tradition, Yvonne Rand was re-establishing order in her Japanese-style home in Muir Beach. She and her husband had just hosted a large group of exiled Tibetan monks in their guest house for several weeks. Since 1984, when she and her husband purchased the land from the Zen Center, this has been one of the functions of their property.

"The way we can support the Tibetan cause is to be a place the Tibetan flag can fly freely," explained Rand, adding that the Chinese takeover of Tibet in 1959 and the subsequent fleeing of the Dali Lama "in some ways was a blessing because it scattered Buddhist tradition all over the world."

Groups from the Gauden Shartse College Monastery and the Gyuto Monastery (monks who chant in three-note harmonies), to name a few, have stayed with Rand, putting on programs and workshops all over the Bay Area.

As comfortable in discussion of the worldly as the divine, Rand discussed the advantages and disadvantages of the full dress of the Buddhist monk. Wearing the robes and

a shaved head invites projections of authority, she noted. It can separate you from normal people. On the other hand, wearing robes is useful in her work with dying persons. "The medical establishment knows how to relate to a priest in a hospital."

"You give up all worldly vanity," she said, "and since we lose 80 percent of our body heat through the head, you learn to manage your body energy. Your head becomes a whole sense organ. You can tell when someone walks in the room just by the change in air currents."

Rand's devotion to the practice of Buddhist meditation began at Stanford, where she met Susuki Roshi, the author of *Zen Mind, Beginner's Mind*. In 1973 she was first ordained as a Zen priest. She is now involved in another ordination ("means to teach fully") ceremony with a small group of students of Susuki Roshi. Roshi is in Minnesota, dying of lymphoma, passing on his knowledge to the end. "Susuki Roshi is teaching me how it's possible to die."

Addiction is a big issue for a lot of people in this culture, she said. "I have found in my own experience and in working with others, the effectiveness of Buddhist practice amazing — especially in combination with 12-step work and more traditional psychotherapy. There's nothing better than working with meditators. The resistance factor is so much lower."

Perfection is the *name* of the squash used, not the degree of excellence, though this soup from the kitchen of Green Gulch's Zen Center is very tasty.

Perfection Squash Soup

Ingredients:

8 cups squash chunks
2 medium yellow onions, diced
3 Tbsp. butter
4 cloves garlic
3/4 tsp. salt
1/2 tsp dried thyme
2 Tbsp. nutritional yeast
4 cups boiling water
1/2 cup cream
1/2 tsp. fresh thyme

Method:

Prepare, peel, cut up squash. In a large soup pot, cook onions in butter with garlic, salt, dried thyme, nutritional yeast. When soft, add squash and water. Cook 40 minutes. Put through a sieve or blender. Add cream. Add fresh thyme, salt and pepper to taste.

CAROL NEGRO

"There's a quality of total dedication to the music. She's very precise and subtle. We all lean forward to listen when she speaks. One night, when we were a bit discouraged, she said, 'Pay great attention to the music and you'll be able to share the genius of these great composers.'"
— member of the West Marin Community Chorus describing director Carol Negro.

On a return visit to Bolinas several years ago, Negro said she kept thinking, "I wish there was a music thing I could do in Bolinas." She picked up the *Hearsay News*, and saw an ad for director of the chorus. Shortly thereafter she became the new director of the West Marin Chorus and Orchestra.

"A chorus is an instrument," she said. "You have to tune a chorus like a violin. The beauty is when everyone is developing and singing absolutely together—every mouth moving from vowel to consonant at the exact same time, so that they start to feel the joy of producing a really pure sound."

A native San Franciscan, Carol Negro directed the San Francisco Children's Chorus for 12 years. Under her direction, the Piedmont Girls' Choir performed in international competitions in China, Newport, RI, and at the Oregon Bach Festival. In 1984 both choirs sang prior to the Super Bowl game at Stanford University.

She founded the Baroque Arts Ensemble, a performance group of 20 singers and 15 instrumentalists, and has developed the West Marin Children's Chorus.

Negro's musical career began at age 10 when she took up the clarinet. At 13, she picked up the bassoon and "fell in love with it." She spent a summer practicing hard and began study with Walter Green, a principal bassoonist with the San Francisco Symphony.

"I was very ambitious," she recalled. "I began auditioning for orchestras. My friends and I played chamber music after school and soon began playing for public events.

"Because of my seriousness, I got a scholarship to Interlochen High School. My most thrilling performance experiences came then. It was wonderful to be immersed in music. All I did was practice. It's amazing what can happen with the focus, proper encouragement and circumstances."

Awarded a scholarship to the University of Cincinnati, Negro graduated with a double degree in theory and bassoon. Returning to San Francisco, her first job was director of the San Francisco Children's Chorus, then under the administration of Landon Young. (Young was the first director of the West Marin Chorus.) "I started conducting and working with children and writing musicals."

Here is a recipe from Carol Negro's kitchen.

Curried Tomato Soup

Ingredients:

1 chopped onion
4 cloves chopped garlic
3 Tbsp. butter
3 Tbsp. curry powder
4 cups chopped tomatoes
1 bay leaf
1 tsp. dried thyme
1 quart chicken broth
1/2 cup white rice

Method:

Sauté one chopped onion and garlic in butter until translucent. Add curry, stir in and simmer until well absorbed. Add tomatoes, spices, broth and rice, and simmer 1-1/2 hrs. Season to taste and serve.

Cold Beet Borsch

Ingredients:

3-1/2 lbs. beets, cleaned and quartered
1 onion, chopped finely
1 tomato, chopped finely
1-1/2 qts. water
1 tsp. caraway
1 tsp. dill
1 tsp. salt
1 tsp. sugar
2 cups chicken broth
juice of 2 lemons

Method:

Cook beets with onion, tomato, dill, caraway, salt and sugar in 1-1/2 quarts of water. Bring to boil and simmer one hour. Pour liquid through strainer, discard solids. Add to liquid 2 cups of chicken broth, and lemon juice. Chill several hours. Before serving, adjust seasoning. Add sliced cucumber and sliced, steamed hot potato, and a dab of sour cream, if desired.

BUD SPANGLER

What a story the charming doll-like house in Bolinas (now named the Blue Heron Inn) could tell. Built sometime before the 1906 earthquake, it has housed a gallery, coffee shop, brunch spot, several elegant dining operations and at least two B&B rooms over the years. It has seen Bolinas from the days of logging through the 1971 oil spill to the present — the hippies, surfers, homeless, DINKs (dual-income-no-kids) and the yups.

With a facelift by owner Bud Spangler, the Blue Heron sparkles invitingly to would-be diners. Its veranda windows glow golden in the evening. Now under new management, Ginger McNew and Suzanna Acevedo have stepped into the kitchen offering elegant dinners, hamburgers for the locals, and homemade desserts. It is open until midnight, for those looking for a place to stop and drink a glass of wine or late-evening coffee.

Bud, Gwen, and their three kids have lived in Bolinas since 1970. "The kids didn't like San Francisco; they wanted to horseback ride and surf," recalled Bud. "So we rented a house in Bolinas. Just as we moved in, the oil spill hit. We didn't know what was going on. It was chaotic." [In 1971, a collossal oil spill off the coast threatened the bird and wildlife of the Bolinas Lagoon. The event became an historical convergence of purpose, Hippies working alongside "rednecks" and Exxon officials, all with the common goal of preventing that oil from entering the lagoon on the next high tide.]

In the meantime, Bud's wife, Gwen has managed The Shop, down the street, offering cafe-deli style fare, Bud's famous chili and homemade soups, salads, entrées and an old-fashioned ice cream soda counter.

Remembering the Gibson House Restaurant (across the street) in its heyday, Bud said, "I was the unofficial manager and bartender when Danny Post had it. She was an excellent cook — a forerunner of Alice Waters' 'California cuisine with a French discipline.' We did the stocks the *correct* way, and she'd use all the local farm products, fresh flowers in salads, fresh fish from the docks. I made salmon paté, and the soups."

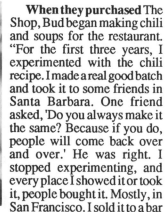

When they purchased The Shop, Bud began making chili and soups for the restaurant. "For the first three years, I experimented with the chili recipe. I made a real good batch and took it to some friends in Santa Barbara. One friend asked, 'Do you always make it the same? Because if you do, people will come back over and over.' He was right. I stopped experimenting, and every place I showed it or took it, people bought it. Mostly, in San Francisco. I sold it to a bar Herb Caen frequented, called the Colosseum II."

I understand that people come from all over the world to taste this chili, which is available sin or con carne, at The Shop in Bolinas. Here's the recipe.

Bud's Famous Three-Bean Chili Con Carne

Ingredients:

1/2 cup black beans
1 cup pinto beans
1/2 cup kidney beans or red beans
2 bay leaves
5 cups peeled canned tomato bits
2 Tbsp. salt
4 cloves garlic, finely chopped
1 Tbsp. oregano
1 Tbsp. crushed hot chilis
2 pinches dried sage
1/4 cup red wine vinegar
1-1/2 cup onions, chopped
1/2 stick butter
1 cup bell pepper, red & green, chopped
1 cup celery, chopped
1/2 cup parsley finely chopped
1 lb. coarse ground lean pork
1-1/2 lb. coarse ground lean beef
1/3 cup chili powder
1/8 cup cumin
3 T. dark brown sugar
1 cake "Ibarra" Mexican chocolate

Method:

Wash dried beans thoroughly. Cover with water and soak at least one hour. Bring to rapid boil, with bay leaves, then simmer until tender; add water if needed. Add: tomatoes, 1/2 garlic, oregano, crushed hot chilis, sage, and red wine vinegar while simmering beans.

In a large frying pan, sauté onions in butter. Stir in bell peppers, celery, parsley and rest of garlic.

In small frying pan, sauté the pork and beef together until all the rawness is gone. Pour the juice from the meat into a skillet. Add chili powder, cumin and dark brown sugar. Bring to a boil and cook for several minutes.

Add these spices to the meat and now add the meat to the simmering beans. Next add all the vegetables to the large pot of beans, simmer on low heat uncovered, stirring every so often. Add Mexican chocolate. If beans become dry, add tomato juice or V-8. Garnish with red and white chopped onions and grated jack and sharp cheddar cheeses.

JOANNA HAIGOOD

The first time I saw Lagunitas dancer/choreographer Joanna Haigood perform, she swooped out onto the stage on a trapeze, floating from one perilous position to another. That was in 1982.

The next time, I watched her slow-motion, languid descent through knotted rope from the top of a 40-foot tree in Washington Square Park. Applause rose from the crowd as she eased to earth. On another occasion she tied off her ropes 50 feet up a giant sequoia in King's Canyon Park for a performance for a Theosophical gathering.

Joanna discovered her flying talents while studying dance in England, through a program at Bard College. She lived next door to a retired woman aerialist of Barnum and Bailey fame; and proved to be a natural.

Since then, her performances won her the Isadora Dance Award, the Bay Guardian Original Local Discovery (GOLDie) award, and a choreography fellowship from the Marin Arts Council. Her innovative and daring performances are drawing crowds to far corners of the Bay Area.

Without even moving, her exotic good looks draw attention, but this intrepid, lithe spirit literally scales walls, effortlessly moving along ledges, moldings, window sills, heaters, and scaffolding in ways you wouldn't dream were possible, at heights that make you cringe. She incorporates aerial flight and suspension with ropes; her work is breathtakingly beautiful. It's often free and often outdoors. You just have to find her.

She works often on commission and in collaboration with artists of other disciplines — she choreographed a piece for the San Francisco ballet company, Lines.

"Theatre Artaud used to be an American Can Company warehouse," explained Joanna. "So I decided to work with the concept of industry. The place was filled with machinery, huge cranes, etc. Dancers started at the second-story bank of windows. I made a glass throne from power insulators, which lit up entirely when touched."

Bees, another performance, was conceived in her studio, an 80-year-old abandoned gymnasium called Building T-952 in the Marin Headlands. In collaboration with bee-keeper and artist Mark Thompson, she transformed the building, casting the windows in wax, bringing in seven hives of honey bees. The two developed the piece, "The Keeping of Bees is Like the Directing of Sunshine," during which Joanna emerged from the hive, covered with honey bees, in barely perceptible motion, exiting by crashing through a window. In the new rays of light, streams of bees followed.

"Breaking through the fear is the most interesting part of the work, to me," said Joanna. "I'm mostly self-taught. I was a cyclone fence specialist. I grew up in New York, and I climbed everything — fences, buildings and telephone poles."

This soup was an integral part of a performance in Washington Square, San Francisco. The aroma of the soup simmering served as the tantalizing backdrop for the dance/drama in which the actors prepared to dine, but never could get to the main course. After the show, both performers and audience were invited to indulge in a cup of this delicious soup.

Joanna's Black Bean Soup

Ingredients:

1-1/2 cup black beans
2-1/2 quarts stock
salt and pepper to taste
3 Tbsp. olive oil
5 large cloves garlic
2 Bay leaves
1/2 tsp. ground cloves
1/2 tsp. ground ginger
1 tsp. cayenne pepper
1-1/2 cubed oranges
2 stalks celery, carrot, chopped
1 onion, chopped

Method:

Place beans in large pot with stock, salt, pepper, and 1 Tbsp. oil. Bring to boil. Simmer until beans are soft. (2-3 hours at least) Sauté vegetables in remaining oil. Add to beans in last hour. Add garlic and spices. Add sweet oranges in last half hour.

ALAN VANN GARDNER

If you peeked into the new Dance Palace at the right moment, you'd chance to find a young man in a long black skirt gracefully turning and rolling soundlessly on yellow mats, with a lot of little ones in white in rapt attention. And if you happen to have a 10- or 11-year-old and live in Point Reyes Station, you'd recognize him as their school teacher.

The man is Alan Gardner — fourth and fifth grade teacher and martial arts teacher and second degree black belt. Teaching, he says, is his calling. And it's not surprising that many of the concepts taught on the mat in his Aikido class work as well in a classroom of kids.

What are those transferable concepts? And for that matter, what is Aikido?

"I want to help kids empower themselves," he began. "So much is how you talk to them .... It's making the classroom a safe place to make mistakes, take risks, get constructive feedback, appreciation and second chances. We work on setting goals, writing outlines... practical things.

"Specifically? Well, one way of empowering yourself is to learn how to follow through and revise your own work. At first I thought teachers should correct papers, but then I realized that they could correct their own work. The kids just needed to know what to look for.

"Instead of telling kids to be quiet, you teach them how to really be quiet — from within

— to be calm inside. We talk about heroes and warriors in social studies. I ask them who their heroes are. Is Rambo a warrior?

"One of the greatest warriors of this century was the founder of Aikido, Morihei Ueshiba. He once said, 'It's not that I don't get thrown off, it's just that I come back so quickly that you can't see it.'"

"Aikido is a method of resolving conflict harmoniously. In practice, you first establish your center and balance. While giving and receiving an attack you notice how and when you get thrown off your center. You practice coming back quickly, in order to do what you need to do. It's a metaphor for life."

Alan's training in Aikido began during summers spent at Naropa Institute in Boulder during his years at Wesleyan College. Working on a master's degree in movement (he was a dance and philosophy major), Alan was naturally drawn to the disciplines of Tai Chi, Aikido, and Lomi body work. He came to Mill Valley to train in Aikido and Lomi bodywork with Wendy Palmer and Richard Heckler.

He attained his teacher certification at Dominican College, and has taught school for three years.

Yosenabe, Japanese for "big pot," is a miso-based fish/seafood soup. While clams, red snapper, tuna and prawns are used in this version, Alan says your favorite fresh fish and seafood will do just fine.

Yosenabe

Ingredients:

3 Tbsp. cold-pressed olive or safflower oil
3 green onions
1/2 lb. mushrooms
2 or 3 shiitake or porcini mushrooms for flavor
3 carrots
6 cloves fresh garlic
1/4 lb. fresh ginger
1/2 lb. clams
1/2 lb. red snapper
1/2 lb. fresh tuna
1/2 lb. prawns
1 lb. tofu cut in 1/2-inch cubes
2-1/2 qts. chicken or vegetable broth
4 heaping Tbsp. red miso
1/2 lb. Japanese soba noodles

Method:

Preparation time: 35 minutes. Makes a big pot.

Chop and saute in cold-pressed olive or safflower oil over medium heat: green onions, 1/2 lb. mushrooms (a few shiitake or porcini add a woody flavor) 3 carrots, thinly sliced.

Mince and add to saute: cloves of fresh garlic and fresh ginger. Clean and add to saute for 5 min: clams, red snapper, fresh tuna and prawns.

Add to saute: tofu cut into cubes.

Add and simmer 10 minutes: chicken or vegetable broth. Dissolve 4 heaping Tbsp. red miso in a little broth and add to soup. In the last 3 minutes of cooking, add Japanese soba noodles.

GEORGE GONZALES

George Gonzales sculpts in stone. Not cement, not brick. Stone. His monolithic works of art will stand the duration of time, in Bolinas where he lives, and around the world. Stonework requires dogged persistence, and a hardy body. George works his body hard, drinks strong coffee and red wine.

He always loved to draw, paint and work with his hands. And when an enthusiastic high school sculpture teacher suggested he enter a competition with his first sculpture of carved marble, he did. He won. And he decided to pursue a career in graphics.

Despite a lucrative graphics career, George was restless. Travelling to Europe, he helped an old friend reconstruct a 12th Century ruin in southern France, with help from "old-country guys." It was his first taste of stone work. "I found it in stone. I had a good eye, a strong body, and I loved it. There's a permanence, a durability in stone — no joints or mortar, just the pure form of fitted stone."

Since then, Gonzales has won national acclaim for his stone sculpture. His creation of the "Wave Organ" through the Exploratorium at the Marin Headlands in 1986 put him on Dan Rather's "Osgood file." The following year he won a design competition for a sculptured fountain for the City of Santa Fe, called Fountain Head Rock.

He was commissioned to create a sculptural entrance to the South Puget Sound Community College, then a project for Sony Corporation in a Tokyo science museum called "listening vessels" and a large sculptured fountain for a private residence and winery in Rutherford. He also won the grand prize at the San Francisco Landscape Garden Show.

Each year George teaches a two-week workshop in stone cutting and building at the Llama Foundation in Taos, New Mexico. He also taught sculpture at Art Park in Lewiston, New York. "I'm a bear of a teacher," he said with a wry grin. "I start 'em out with the hardest stone and the dullest chisels."

A source of genuine pride to Gonzales is his "freelance petroglyphic graffiti" — stone-chiseled spirals in rocks on four continents. One, in Baja, he chiseled on the vertical face of a rock 40-feet up. Just for fun.

"It is slow tedious work. It's like a brotherhood and you have to be crazy to do it," said George. "I met these two old stoneworker partners and noticed each was missing a thumb on one hand. One was hammering and the other holding a chisel one day. The hammerer missed and severed his partner's thumb completely. At that point the former placed his own hand down and said, "Cut mine off too or I'll never be able to look at you again."

Here is a recipe from George's Basque grandmother.

Barcelona-style Crab Cioppino

Ingredients:

2 large cans whole tomatoes
2 heads minced garlic
3 medium chopped onions
 4 clove stems
2 Bay leaves
8 live crabs (chop in 1/2, then clean, saving body shell, removing legs)
3 lbs. medium shrimp
3 lbs. live clams
3 lbs. sea bass (white fish)
Mussels, scallops, etc.
olive oil
1 bunch parsley, minced

Method:

Put olive oil in a pot (number 1). Add garlic and onion, turning until light brown over low heat. Add tomatoes. Add clove and Bay. Let simmer for 2 hours.

Stock: Start another pot (pot number 2) with 1/2 gallon water heating. Throw in crab shells and 2 whole bodies (legs removed). Add 1 chopped onion, celery, 1 whole head garlic. Simmer alongside tomato mixture. This is used to dilute the soup.

In extra-large pot number 3, put olive oil. Add 2 heads more chopped garlic and 1/2 bunch chopped parsley. Throw in the rest of crab (6 de-legged bodies) and turn, continuously. The crab will turn red in about 20 minutes. Then throw clams in, turn for a few minutes. Pour on tomato sauce, stir in. Now throw in sea bass, shrimp, still in shell and cook for 10-15 minutes. Use stock to thin soup to desired consistency. Serve with French bread and red wine. Garnish with parsley.

JUDY NORTH

Deep in the redwoods of San Geronimo Valley is the studio and home of artist Judy North. Her paintings are combinations of watercolor, gold and silver leaf, oil stick, lacquer and acrylic on gessoed paper. Theatre, feminism, politics, history, her own Scotch-Irish heritage, and personal psychological delvings have had strong effects on her work. "I'm painting to reveal my feelings," she said. "These are my navigations and my observations."

Stained glass was her first medium, while in her early years growing up in Los Angeles. During her marriage to Ronnie Davis (then director of the San Francisco Mime Troupe) she grew fascinated with the theatre, and designed sets while raising three children. With their divorce, she moved to Vermont to teach stained-glass technique at Bennington College for five years.

Then came one of those "life changes" she often refers to. She returned to the Bay Area, remarried, and began to paint.

"I had this little book of Scottish tartans that I loved," she said. "Those tartans told the ancient truths of the culture. They told you who you were in a tribal society. From 400 yards off you could tell who a person was — whether to run or to greet the person." She painted these extraordinary tartans for the next two years.

The tartans evolved into portraits. "I began to study my grandmother, Eliza Ingram Campbell, and her first husband Harold. They lived in Minnesota. He had a strange habit of taking the car out late on wintry nights, driving as fast as he could and then stepping on the brakes, doing 360-degree out-of-control turns.

"I did 11 pieces of him. I was looking past the image of the man I saw in the photo. I wanted to see who was behind the photo."

A photo of her mother, a wild headstrong girl, captured during a costume party aboard a ship to Europe, was the next point of inspiration for North. A demonic, androgynous figure in the corner of the photo caught her attention. She began a series titled "Madame Moustach."

North's paintings have provocative titles, such as "More Than Meets the Eye" and "It Furthers One to Cross the Great Waters," and "Know Thyself." Her themes have been called "tempestuous," "restless," "inviting" and "perplexing". Always they are spiritual investigations, and walk the line between visual, almost religious extravagance, and the painterly contrast of unfinished textures, and surprises.

Most recently North has shown her work at the San Francisco Museum of Modern Art, the Contemporary Arts Forum in Santa Barbara and at the California State University Art Gallery, Stanislaus. She received a Marin Arts Council Grant in the Visual Arts and is teaching at UC Davis.

For something warm and satisfying within, on a foggy evening in West Marin, Judy North offers this savory fare:

Mussel and Turban Snail Chowder

Ingredients:

2-3 dozen mussels
2 dozen snails
1 large clove garlic
splash white wine
1/4 lb chopped salt pork
1 medium onion
2 cups water
salt, pepper
2-3 diced potatoes
2 cups whole milk
1 can evaporated milk
2 Tbsp. flour

Method:

Put on a large pot of boiling water. Add a clove of garlic to water and splash of white wine. Drop mussels and snails in boiling water and simmer for 8-10 minutes. When mussels open their shells, take the pot off the heat, drain off water, saving the savory cooking water, straining off flotsam and jetsum, cool and remove from shells.

In a large sturdy pot, fry chopped salt pork until golden brown. Set pork aside. Chop and sauté onion in the pork fat. Add 2 cups of stock from cooking shellfish, salt, pepper and potatoes. Simmer 20 to 30 minutes until potatoes are tender. Mix together the whole and evaporated milk. Blend in the flour. Add to the pot. Add cooked mussels and snails and heat. Serve.

RAY BELDNER

What Have We Got To Lose? was the provocative name of a series of art exhibits for summer 1990 by Gallery Route One, the cooperative gallery in Point Reyes Station. The series of lectures and exhibits was intended to illustrate the relationship between the environment and the artist .... and everybody else who cares for the earth.

When artist Ray Beldner, who frequents Tomales Bay and the West Marin coast, heard that Gallery Route One was accepting proposals for a sculpture at Millerton Point on Tomales Bay, he started thinking and came up with an idea.

The proposal Beldner submitted to the gallery conceded, "There is a dilemma in trying to create an artwork in a place such as this. Almost anything built or placed upon this site will be overwhelmed by the brooding presence of the bay, the sweeping expanse of the sky and the flocks of waterfowl that live in this fragile ecosystem.... I couldn't help but regret that I was allowed to even walk in the park."

On the other hand, Beldner recognized man's intrusive presence in nature and how much a contemporary person's experience of nature is manipulated. "On any path, I realize I am destined to see exactly what people want me to see. It's a trade-off. Going off the path would destroy the natural beauty. So we have to standardize people's experience of nature."

The Nature of Experience, Ray Beldner's sculpture, which was inspired by the state park at Millerton Point, was a mowed path which attempted to guide walkers on a "blatantly artifi-

cial," triangular path across the park. At the first stop on the path, a steel box emanated calls of osprey and crows and other birds.

The second point was on the edge of the bluffs where the walker can look out over Tomales Bay. The view, however, was interrupted by two metal rectangles on posts at eye level. Hikers looking through peep holes in the metal signposts could view a map of the area. The third stop was a six-foot-high, neat stack of real estate "for sale" signs, impaled on a metal pole. This "commemorated the triumph of this small plot of land from development," said Beldner.

The fourth and last stop was a bench, where the visitor might rest and consider what importance Millerton Point has for them.

It's an interesting issue Beldner has raised — this paradox of man and the environment. We've screwed it up so badly, it makes me cringe to think how man is going to set about "righting" his damage. Will it be by marching out into nature en masse, even for environmental art openings? Is it inevitably human nature to carve our initials on everything? Couldn't we just leave it alone?

On the other hand, what is man, if not nature, and better to be reminded of our hefty impact on the ecosystem, than to continue in our ignorance.

Ray Beldner received his Bachelor of Fine Arts in painting at the San Francisco Art Institute, and his MFA in sculpture from Mills College. He is pretty good in the kitchen, too. He says this recipe, when cooked down becomes thick, almost like a pea soup, and, though it may seem a strange combination, is delicious. Here's the recipe.

Carrot-Orange Soup

Ingredients:

3 Tbsp. butter
1 yellow onion
1 lb. carrots, peeled and sliced
1 tsp. salt
1/4 cup fresh parsley, minced
1 Bay leaf
1 tsp. fresh minced thyme
8 cups water
peel of 1/2 orange, finely minced
juice of one orange
1/4-1/2 cup cream

Method:

Melt butter in stock pot. Add onion and cook, stirring for five minutes. Add carrots and salt, stirring and cooking 10 more minutes. Add herbs and water and bring to boil. Reduce heat to maintain slow bubbling and cook 25 minutes. Remove soup from heat, liquefy in a blender until smooth. Optional: Strain soup through a fine sieve back into pot (but it's thicker and richer if you don't). Return soup to the stove and add the orange peel, orange juice and cream, stirring over low heat to combine. Turn off heat when soup gets hot, cover and let stand for 10-15 minutes. Garnish with fresh herbs and/or a dollop of cream.

Lydia Smith

It was the summer of 1925 when young Lydia Smith, a graduate of San Francisco State, was hired to teach in the little one-room Pierce Point School.

Today at 86, she lives in her home overlooking the Bolinas Lagoon; she's bright and alive, with an eye on the elections and local politics and a sharp memory that goes back and back. She taught for 12 and a half years at the Bolinas School, retiring at 66; she may well be the oldest oldtimer in town, she says.

Mrs. Smith recalled her first trip to Bolinas by stage from Sausalito which she took to visit a friend's ranch in Paradise Valley. She remembers being introduced to her would-be husband Sherman who only grunted, upon their first meeting. "But later I learned what a kind, generous, perfect gentleman he really was," she added. (They were married after her two years of schoolteaching in Pierce Point.) Sherman's grandmother rode around in a horse drawn sulky and raced on the beach, she recalled.

The following are written memories of her first days in Pierce Point:

"Upon arriving at Hamlet via the narrow gauge train, I was met by Mr. Jack Gallagher, who ferried me across Tomales Bay in his boat. We anchored at his dock and proceeded to walk the short distance up the hill to the huge farm house.

"We were met by Mrs. Gallagher carrying the baby and accompanied by their other two charming little daughters, Gladys and Elaine. Immediately I knew I would enjoy this friendly family."

(The Gallaghers ran a dairy ranch, and hired a dozen ranch hands who lived in buildings on the grounds. Lydia was shown to her upstairs room with a grand view of Tomales Bay to the north.)

"School started, and I found it satisfying to teach a group of youngsters whose former teachers had them well prepared for their grade levels. (There were two rows of desks, a woodstove, and an anteroom for storage and wood.) I'm not sure I remember all the names but there were Viliciches, Matkoviches, the Pensotti sisters and Gladys Gallagher. I've always appreciated having had the opportunity to teach in that tiny school.

"At the ranch, one of the milkers took a vacation, a trip to Italy. He came back with a bride. She was a lovely bride, but not a cook. When Mrs. Gallagher suddenly became ill and went to the hospital, she left a recipe for corn soup which I made for the family table.

"The new bride, in the meantime, would put together a huge piece of home-raised beef and a variety of vegetables to make the daily soup for the men's (milkers) dining room, but she'd start so late it wasn't half done for the milkers at the end of the day. I suggested she start earlier, but she didn't speak a word of English, nor I a word of Italian. I presume her husband helped her understand because there was an improvement. The working men were gracious, never complaining, but they were good at making jokes about the situation.

"Gladys and I picked large luscious blackberries each evening for dessert and served them with plenty of Holstein cream. When Mrs. Gallagher returned home, happiness returned to a group of grateful people at the farm."

Lydia Smith's Country Corn Soup

Ingredients:

1-16 oz. can creamed yellow corn
1/2 cup water
2 rounded Tbsp. butter
 Salt to taste
A little pepper
1/4 Bay leaf
1 pint of milk (or less)

Method:

Put creamed corn (approximately 2 cups) through a strainer until even the kernel hearts crush, leaving only the hulls or skins for disposal. Place strained corn in open pot. Add 1.2 cup water, salt, pepper, 2 Tbsp. butter and bay leaf. Simmer for a few minutes. Add milk, according to thickness you desire. Siimmer for ten minutes. Stir very often to prevent soup from sticking to bottom of pan. Remove Bay leaf. It's the Bay leaf which creates the distinctive taste. Serves. 6.

MARGARET FRINGS KEYES

The Enneagram Cats of Muir Beach is the provocative title of a newly published book by coastal author and psychotherapist, Margaret Frings Keyes. When it landed on my desk, I thought, "Oh, a children's book complete with lovable cat characters."

Well, it's not exactly a child's story. Ostensibly an enchanting tale of the romance between Aida and Tom-Tom, two cats who live in Muir Beach, *Cats* is a richly layered study of personality types. There are nine types as identified by an ancient Sufi system known as the Enneagram. (Sufism is an Islamic form of mysticism.)

"This Enneagram system," explained Keyes, "is a system the average person can use powerfully. It's a way that people can better understand what's happening to them."

A Jungian therapist for 35 years and a graduate in social work from the University of Chicago, Keyes has conventional credentials in the field of psychotherapy. But she is eclectic in her study and use of varying methods; she's studied Gestalt therapy with Fritz Perls, Transactional Analysis, and psychodrama. In the 1970s, Keyes first encountered Sufism and the Enneagram's descriptions of nine personality types.

In *Cats*, she has "given away" the work she has been doing for 35 years. "I think I have a skill in using regular talk — not esoteric jargon — to get these ideas out," she explained. "That's why I wrote *Cats*. I want to pass the work on to someone new to carry on."

In many ways, *Cats* is a logical sequel to her previous book, titled *Emotions and the Enneagram, Working Through Your Shadow Life Script*. In this book, she has synthesized Jung's concept of the shadow self, the Enneagram and modern psychological theory. She tells how to recognize our own particular responses to the world.

But in *Cats* she lets the characters themselves tell the story. You may recognize people you know in these felines There are references to stories such as Abelard and Heloise or Archie and Mehitabel. There is "Silky Sue" who gives expert advice on the care and training of cat owners.

There is "Chester" who can't decide whether to catch butterflies or admire them. In one section, while on a quest to find the wizard Fogarty in a Miwok midden, the cats are put under a "trans-induction," as prescribed by psychotherapist Milton Ericson.

Keyes said much of the book arose from her walks in Muir Beach with a longterm friend. "I'd tell him the story as far as I'd gotten, and he'd come up with some challenge or something to push me. We laughed through the whole making of this book. We still do," she said, glancing at her lovely Siamese cat named Aida.

Here is Keyes's recipe for a hot soup on a foggy summer night on the coast of Marin. Your cat will probably try to convince you she will die if she doesn't get some shrimp:

Bouillabaisse

Ingredients:

1/3 cup minced garlic
1-2 onions, slivered
1 cup sliced green onions
1 lb. shelled shrimp
2-3 cups chicken broth
1-2 Bay leaves
1/3 cup olive oil
1-1/2 lb. shark or swordfish
1 lb. clams in shells
1 lb. mussels
1/2-1 lb. bay or sea scallops or any combination
of rock cod, salmon, sea bass, etc. that looks
and smells fresh in the morning market.

Method:

Cook garlic and onions in olive oil until limp, stirring 12-15 minutes. Add chicken broth, simmer 10 minutes longer. Add larger chunks of fish. When these begin to become slightly opaque, add clams and mussels. Serve (when the shells open) over a slice of pan-toasted French bread in each soup bowl. This is great with spinach salad and a rich dessert — such as sliced bananas and dates drizzled with thick cream and left over night in the fridge. Serves 8.

BREADS & MUFFINS

DAVID SCHANAKER

It hurts. You start to get out of bed and your back painfully reminds you of yesterday's ambitious gardening project. That's the bad news.

The good news: Dr. David Schanaker, of Stinson Beach, has opened a chiropractic practice, in an office adjacent to the Stinson Gym on Highway 1. His wide grin, and bouncy stride exude robust well-being. And his confident, calm bedside manner melts anxieties away.

"I use both traditional and non-traditional methods, in a wholistic approach to health," said Schanaker. "I give a regular medical exam, and do blood work, sending samples to the lab through the Family Practice in Bolinas. And I also use applied kinesiology, acupressure, polarity therapy, diet surveys, herbal remedies, spinal adjustments, exercises ... and common sense."

Born in Sonoma, Schanaker spent much of his youth in Marin. He got his degree from Western States Chiropractic College in Portland, racing bicycles when he wasn't studying. Before coming to Stinson, Schanaker practiced at a sports clinic called Spectrum in Corte Madera for 3-1/2 years, but was dissatisfied with the short amount of time he could spend with each client. He moved to Stinson with partner and dancer Erica.

"About half of my clients come to me with job-related injuries — whiplash, falls or back pains, joint or muscle aches and pains," said Schanaker. "The other half want a natural solu-

tion to a chronic problem, such as indigestion, or high blood pressure. They want to make changes in their health status."

In ever-increasing demand, Schanaker also works with dancers and athletes, giving programs on care of the body in training — nutritional needs, care of the feet, back and specific body parts, as well as keeping the mind balanced.

Shanaker keeps himself fit and healthy "working out in the gym next door about three times a week for general toning." He's started training in Aikido, practices yoga, and meditates regularly, with breath work.

But his eyes lit up as he confessed, "I have passionately fallen in love with surfing. In surfing you are very intimate with the water. It's very Zen; you paddle out and sit out there on the water and look out to sea, watching the movement of the water. It's a wonderful sport, and the aerobic exercise is outstanding."

There are two books which Schanaker recommends, saying, "These sum up how I feel about diet." They are *Staying Healthy with the Seasons* by Elson Hass, MD, and *Diet for a New America* by John Robbins. "I would advocate a thoughtfully put together vegetarian diet," he said.

"This recipe," said Schanaker, "is from my friend and patient, Barbara Kahn, and will be included in her new cookbook.

Real Corn Muffins

Ingredients:

1 cup yellow corn meal
1 cup whole wheat flour
1/3 cup soy flour
2 tsp. baking powder
2 tsp. safflower oil
1 egg
1 cup fresh corn
1-1/2 cup apple juice
1/4 cup maple syrup

Method:

Preheat oven to 400 degrees. Combine corn meal, whole wheat flour, soy flour and baking powder. In a bowl, beat egg into oil, adding apple juice and maple syrup. Add fresh corn. Mix in dry ingredients a little at a time. Pour into oiled and floured muffin tins. Bake for 20-23 minutes.

BILL SCOTT

The Parkside Cafe, tucked away from Highway 1 in Stinson Beach is a cheery little family-run restaurant, perfect for a get-away breakfast or lunch. It's not fancy fare. It's simply good downhome food in a downhome atmosphere.

You can invent your own omelette or take a suggestion from the cook, Bill Scott, who says confidently, "I don't know of anyone who makes a better omelette."

The accompanying toast is so good, you'll want to take home a loaf of their homemade bread, baked on the premises from a family recipe made from freshly ground wheat berries. Bran muffins in four variations, coffee cake, cookies and pastries as well as bread tempt from the display counter. But the real temptation is the freshly made cinnamon rolls, made each day by early morning baker, Diana Morell.

The Scott family bought the cafe in 1982, and Bill, with a bit of experience cooking in college, and a whole lot of certainty about what he likes to eat, agreed to take the job as line-cook.

"The food is designed to be as simple as possible. The secret to the taste of food is using good ingredients — and don't burn things. We don't serve a lot of sauces. It's a no-frills, downhome restaurant. That's the way we want people to feel — at home here."

Truly it is a mix of styles. They serve traditional fare— hamburger and fries — but if you order a salad, you'd think you were at a fancy cafe, when a huge plate of assorted fresh greens, artfully decorated with beets, and crumbled blue cheese arrives.

Barbara Scott, Bill's mother grows a vegetable garden on a plot of land adjacent to the restaurant. The cafe serves her fresh, homegrown vegetables all summer long. "It's amazing how much produce you can get from a 30' by 20' garden," said Bill. "In the summer we don't order any lettuce. That's a lot."

Diana Morell, manager of Stinson Beach's Ocean Court Motel, is the current cinnamon roll maker for the Parkside Cafe. The recipe, she says, has been slightly changed from the original one passed down called "Cinny's Rolls."

She makes 10 dozen of these in the time most folks would make one. They are surprisingly light and sweet, but not too sweet. Diana says the secret to making these rolls is to be mindful not to handle the dough too much. You need a delicate touch, since the recipe calls for an instant (fast) yeast.

Here we offer you the chance to recreate the Scott family's Raisin Walnut Bread and try your hand at Cinny's rolls in your own kitchen.

(Note: For people who fail at this, these might be the reasons: Using water that's too hot kills the yeast. Letting bread rise where it's too warm, or for too long before putting in oven. It should be rising just to top of pan.)

Scott Family Raisin Walnut Bread

Ingredients:(Makes 4 loaves)

4 cups warm water
1/3 cup oil
1/4 cup yeast
1-1/2 tsp. salt
2/3 cup brown sugar
2 cups walnuts
half & half whole wheat/ white flour
6 cups raisins

Method:

Beat briskly together the water, yeast, brown sugar and enough flour to make a "muddy" texture for 1 minute. Cover sponge for 1/2 hour.

Add oil, salt, walnuts, raisins. Mix, adding more flour to make it dough consistency. Knead. (By hand, 25 minutes, by Cuisinart, 8-10 minutes) Cover. Let rise until double in warm place. Punch down with fingers. Cut into 4 loaf sizes. Let sit another 10 minutes. Last kneading: Knead each portion until when a finger punched in, dough springs it back. Bake at 350 for 40 minutes or when bottom of pan sounds hollow when knocked, and there's no give in the top of the crust.

Diana's Cinnamon Rolls

Ingredients:

4 cups warm water
1 cup brown sugar
2-1/2 oz. of fast activating yeast
8 cups white flour, sifted (The Cafe uses a fine, gluten flour which works nicely)
1 cup corn or safflower oil
2 eggs
1-1/2 tsp. salt
1/4 cup blackstrap molasses
4 cups whole wheat flour
1 cup melted butter
1/2 cup cinnamon
2 cups brown sugar
currants
optional: nuts, jellied fruits, raisins, other dried fruit

For glaze:
1 cup powdered sugar
3 Tbsp. milk

Method:

Mix water & sugar together until well dissolved, add yeast and mix well. Sprinkle in the flour. It'll become a smooth sticky substance. Let this sit and rise in a warm room until double. It will "pouf" up, in an hour. Don't let it get too big.

Now work in the oil and the eggs, until well mixed. Add salt and molasses and continue to mix .Add flour, kneading and working until it looks like bread dough. Knead it well, then let sit and rise again until doubled.

Next, roll out this dough on a floured counter to 1/2 inch thickness. Paint melted butter on dough. Mix cinnamon and sugar together; sprinkle this and currants and/or nuts, on top.

Roll up dough, being delicate, making it into a tube, (fist size in diameter). Slice with a perforated knife, to pieces 1 " thick. Wait 5 min. Bake at 325-350 only 10-15 min. on upper shelf, since the sugary bottoms burn easily.

For glaze:

Mix and adjust proportions until you have a pourable, but thick icing. Drip this over the cinnamon rolls while they are still hot.

CYNDI BARRETT

Pipe holders of the Native American tradition do not give interviews, as a rule. In fact, Lakota Indian Cyndi Barrett thought about it some time before agreeing. Her path, that of the Sioux, is one of the oldest teachings. Having taken the sacrificial vows of the pipe, she goes where she is needed. And she has come to Bolinas.

"We try to live a humble life," explained Barrett. "We don't want to be known as magicians. We are private in our ways. It's not so much who I am, rather, what I teach ..."

Barrett wasn't born a pipe carrier. "I was born Indian, outside Dallas, on a large ranch with a big family. We raised horses and cattle and worked the land. We knew them, but we didn't practice Indian ways. My grandmother slipped in the teachings. She's a big part of who I am today."

The sweat lodge is a key part of Barrett's program: "Entering the lodge is to surrender; to literally go into the unknown, the darkness, in ignorance," she explained. "We go into the lodge with a question. Then, by letting go, we move on, to a new understanding...It teaches us to live in our hearts, not our heads. It's a dynamic and

powerful way to pray. That's what the sweat lodge is about.

"I have seen people move through emotional and physical changes very quickly. I do counseling and one-on-one sweats, working with them before we go into the sweat. And almost without fail, when they come out, there's a clarity, a knowing of what they need to do next."

Every part of the ceremony is significant, from the cutting and bending of 16 willow saplings (the frame of the lodge, positioned in four directions), to the fire and heating of the stones outside the lodge. "We thank the trees for giving their life, in order to give back someone else's."

Inside the sweat lodge, red hot rocks are brought into the center of the lodge through the blanketed entrance. Prayers to the earth, the spirits, and "all my relations" (O Mitak oyasin, [O mee tak kwee ahh see] are spoken in a circle, as the steamy heat rises. "But all sweat ceremonies are done a little differently," she explained. "You see, we don't lead the sweats. Each one is done the way the spirits want it to be done. For 24 hours before a ceremony, I get very still and ask for clarity. I meditate and pray with my pipe until the moment I crawl in the lodge. Some are afraid of sweats, but this is a gentle, beautiful path. It's about finding God through love."

Here is a Native American Indian recipe to try:

Hush Puppies

Ingredients:

2 cups cornmeal
2/3 -1 cup milk
1 tsp. salt
2 large eggs, beaten
2 tsp. baking powder
1 chopped small onion

Method:

Mix milk and eggs in a large bowl; add the cornmeal, baking powder, salt and onions. Drop by tbsp into 1" hot oil in skillet. Fry til golden brown, drain.

JOHN McCHESNEY & JOANNE WALLACE

Breakfast conversations at the Tomales Country Inn (formerly the Byron Randall Guest House) have probably always been scintillating fare, and new owners John McChesney and JoAnne Wallace are continuing the tradition of the "salon," with a decidedly "All Things Considered" flair.

John is now working as a freelance journalist after 10 years with National Public Radio in Washington, D.C. He built NPR's network of foreign news reporters "from scratch," and also managed the national desk and its reporters. He is responsible for "Morning Edition's" addition and for much of the brilliance of "All Things Considered." Now he writes on economic or environmental themes for the network.

JoAnne is a consultant for public radio broadcast systems, having 20 years of experience in program directing and public affairs for stations such as WYSO at Antioch College in Ohio, KPFA in Berkeley, classical station WGBH in Boston and NPR in Washington.

"Last Saturday morning, I ran a piece I did on an LA Insurance broker on 'Morning Edition' for our guests at breakfast," said John. "I'm afraid they were a captive audience, but a willing one. The conversations are often very lively and last all morning long. Some very interesting people come through here."

McChesney and Wallace are quick to credit prior owner Byron Randall for the stream of interesting folks who still visit the 100-year-old guest house. Randall lives in the small cottage next to the guest house, where he paints every day. Randall ran the inn for years on the honor system, which required there to be notes everywhere to instruct guests — "Leave your check here," "Help yourself to cooking utensils," etc. Since John and JoAnne actually live in the house, they now answer the door themselves, serve breakfast and converse with guests. The number of Randall's original paintings may have thinned, but they can still be found throughout the house. And Randall's famous hand-powered potato-masher collection hangs in a room just off the kitchen.

They don't feel cut off from the world in Tomales. Rather, they have worked harder here than when they were in Washington. In the year since they assumed ownership of the inn, John's assignments have taken him to the timber country of Tongass National Forest, back to Washington, to a Toyota plant in Fremont, and to a hospital in Oakland.

JoAnne has been able to do much of her work over the phone and by mail. "The quiet and utter simplicity is refreshing," said JoAnne. "Folks in town have been very friendly and helpful. But I think if we lived here 50 years, we'd still be known as 'newcomers.' That's okay. It's just the way it is."

To stay in touch with the world from Tomales isn't hard. They read five newspapers a day, (*NY Times, LA Times* and *Wall Street Journal* for starters,) own a Fax machine, a computer with a modem and of course, a radio.

John cooks breakfasts for guests at the Tomales Country Inn and on special occasions whips up these delicious "labor intensive" scones.

Breakfast Scones

Ingredients:

2 cups flour
1/2 tsp. baking soda
2 tsp. baking powder
3/4 tsp. nutmeg
1/2 tsp salt
1 stick butter (1/2 cup)
2 Tbsp. sugar
1 egg yolk
3/4 cup buttermilk
1 cup raisins

Method:

Preheat oven to 375 degrees. In a food processor, combine flour, baking soda, nutmeg, and salt. Add butter in small pieces mixing until it's a grainy cornmeal consistency. Remove and put in a bowl.

Whip together egg yolk and buttermilk. Add sugar and raisins. Add this to flour mixture. Knead 10-12 times. It will be very sticky, so flour hands well. Flatten into a mound 6 inches in diameter. Cut into wedges. It will yield six nice-sized scones. Scoop onto cookie sheet. Bake 20-25 minutes or until golden brown.

BARBARA KAHN

It was a shock for Inverness resident Barbara Lakshmi Kahn to learn that her cholesterol level was far too high. The blood serum reading of 270 she received at a health fair was probably due to the buttered popcorn she had eaten the night before, she reasoned. But when a second reading confirmed the accuracy of the first, she decided to do something about it.

"I went to a doctor to find out how I could reduce my cholesterol level," she explained. "Genetics is a large factor in this tendency, and since my father had suffered a heart attack, I wanted to do everything I could."

Kahn began her research, learning about cholesterol. She immediately began a diet low in saturated fat, and high in fiber. That's right, bye bye cheese, butter, eggs and choice cuts of beef.

The results were dramatic. In less than three months, she reduced her cholesterol level 100 points, back into a safe, healthy range. Accepting the ongoing challenge, she discovered tasty alternatives to replace those fatty culprits and still satisfy her six-foot husband, John Robbins. And in the course of changing their eating habits, she wrote down the recipes. She still makes enchiladas, dips, and sauces, but now items like soy milk and soy cheese can be found on her refrigerator shelves.

Better known to many as a painter, Kahn has put aside her painting easel for a while to work on a cookbook featuring 150 low cholesterol, high-fiber and low-salt recipes. The book will be titled

Cooking Organic, Delicious ways to preserve and prepare organic foods year round. "It will also include tips on storing, sprouting, freezing, dehydrating and canning food," she said.

Kahn has always grown her own vegetables and is concerned that produce be organic. "I can now be 90 percent organic year round," she said proudly. She uses a food hydrator to dry tomatoes, peaches, nectarines, apples, even hot peppers, a coffee grinder for spices and a food processor, for chopping and canning.

She loves to hike in the countryside, collecting wild edibles — mushrooms, herbs and flowers. In the colorful salad she had prepared were Calendula leaves, chickweed, pansy flowers, forget-me-nots, wild radish and kale blossoms. But not wild watercress. "Watercress grows in streams," she warned, "and sometimes carries a liver fluke from cattle and animals in the area. I don't recommend eating it raw, unless it's from a store. The fluke gradually deteriorates the liver."

"Cholesterol is a necessary ingredient in our bodies, and is produced by the body itself," she explained. "It only becomes our adversary when it is in excess, when arteries become lined with deposits, decreasing blood flow, causing heart disease."

"Having bountiful energy, physical fitness, mental alertness, dexterity, mobility, spirit and a strong immune system is part of my live-to-100 philosophy," said Kahn with a broad grin.

Here is a low cholesterol recipe from Barbara Kahn's cookbook:

Low Cholesterol Breakfast Cake

Dry ingredients:

1 cup walnuts
3/4 cup whole wheat flour
1 cup raisins
1/4 cup soy flour
1 apple cored, chopped
1 cup oat bran
1 cup chopped dried fruit
1/2 cup wheat bran
grated orange peel
2 Tbsp. lecithin granules

Wet ingredients:

1 egg
2 Tbsp. cinnamon
2 Tbsp. canola oil
1 cup soy milk
1/2 cup honey
2 tsp. non-aluminum baking powder
1 tsp. almond extract

Method:

Combine and stir dry ingredients together until fruit is coated with flour.

Blend wet ingredients until smooth, and stir into dry mixture. Mix together thoroughly. Spoon into oiled 9-inch baking dish. Sprinkle witu brown sugar. Bake at 375 degrees for 30-35 minutes.

Allow to cool, and serve.

JODY FOSS

With shocking-blue eyes, Tomales muletrekker Jody Foss has a radiance that doesn't come from watching TV. No wonder. She'd only been home a few days from a 54-day, 560-mile trek, accompanied only by her three mules, Sarah, Mavis, and Brighty (plus Reba, given to her near the end of her trip).

"We picked up the Pacific Crest Trail near Bend, crossing Eastern Oregon to Virginia City, Nevada," she explained. The Town of Tomales sponsored her trip. Sally Parks of the Country Delights Deli helped raise money and "gave me this enormous sausage as I left."

Foss recalled some of the moments that made the trip worth all the effort. One was being 8,800 feet up in the South Warner Wilderness area where one can almost see to the sea. There's Mt. Shasta, a giant pink cone in the sunset, and east, you can see clear across Nevada.

"There's a synchronicity that happens out there after a while," Foss said. "I almost know when things are going to happen ... little things are so much more important; people so dear."

Foss refuses to carry a gun, saying, "I think guns just attract danger. All I carry is a Swiss army knife... But there is an element of danger." One evening, she was "foolish with the Coleman fuel" as she was making camp, and burned her hand badly. She bandaged the wound herself, but realized it was serious. "The next day, following the trail down to the road, an EMT drove up and told me he was there to treat my hand. Apparently, through the Forest Service hotline, people knew about my accident," she said.

"At one point I was up on dry ranch land of Eastern Oregon. I was out of water for two days, and I was worried. But that night, this Texas cowboy walked into my camp with five gallons of water, and said, ' I brought you some water for your mules.' Word had passed about the 'mule lady' coming down the cattle drive trail, and these guys happened to be at this satellite bunkhouse, miles away."

She was befriended by a white kitten for part of her trip, who rode in a bucket up front on her saddle. But in town one day the kitten was hit by a car and died. "I couldn't believe how much that kitten meant to me, even after only a few days," she said, sadly.

"The last two days were the hardest of the trip. I thought we were real close, and as a kind of celebration, I dumped out my water bags. Right then a cold wind came up, and I realized we still had six miles to go. A guy told us of a short cut across the Truckee River over a train trestle. It's always trouble when people say, 'Go this way. It'll save you a couple of miles.' With a pack of mules, we had to bushwack. I fell in the Truckee River, which is very polluted right there, and we slept under I-80."

This was Foss' sixth mule-trek. It has been documented in a slide show, the third in a series, called "The Sagebrush Story, Mules Across America." She's been shown on KQED, and she's toured with two previous slide shows. The soundtrack is a collage of music and interviews of old-timers, responding to her inquiry as to what they feel is important in life.

Jody's Off Trail Bread Recipe

Ingredients:

4 cups lukewarm water
1/2 cup brown sugar
4 Tbsp. fresh baking yeast granules
unbleached white flour
whole wheat flour
salt

Fillings:

1) Fresh rosemary, garlic and onions sautéed in butter
2) Salsa, garlic and fresh cilantro
3) Fresh tarragon and garlic
4) Parmesan cheese and oregano leaves
5) Cinnamon, orange marmalade and butter

Method:

Mix sugar and yeast into the warm water in a big bowl. Let activate on top of a warm oven for 10 minutes. Mix in flour until kneading consistency is accomplished.

Mix in salt to taste. Knead bread until your forearms are aching (for me about 10 minutes). Leave to rise, 45 minutes to 1 hour on top of warm stove.

Roll out with a rolling pin on a clean table until dough is one-inch thick. Then you can cover the dough with a variety of delicious fillings.

Roll up dough, close ends, and bake until when knocked, it sounds hollow and it turns golden brown.

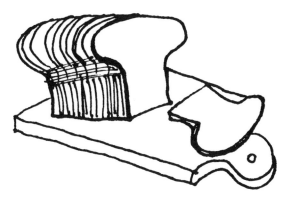

DEBRA RUFF & BRIDGET SAWYER

Business has been brisk at the new Bovine Bakery since its opening on the main street in Point Reyes Station. Proprietors Debra Ruff and Bridget Sawyer say they've been doubling and tripling their recipes, and they're still selling out by the end of the day.

The two surprisingly young and pretty women bakers (I don't know what I expected, grandma, maybe?) stood at a large work table between two 68-pound blocks of butter, moving back and forth from refrigerators, hands in constant motion as we spoke. These are the wives of the Hog Island Oystermen (up the road in Tomales) who've put their heads together to find a way to keep themselves happily employed on *this* side of the hill, with their families, (each is mother of a small child) and contribute to the community as well. Because they've both been in the food business since they were 15, they opted for a hometown storefront to display their baking talents.

Determined to do it right, they trained with a friend and French pastry bakery owner in Santa Cruz (Kelly's French Pastries) over the last year and a half, who helped them avoid the pitfalls of starting a new business and gave lessons in the labor-intensive croissant dough-making.

Debra has years of experience in the catering business, coordinating weddings and parties; her specialties are the French pastries — plain, almond, chocolate, and ham and cheese croissants, bear claws, morning sticky buns. Before she began the new bakery, she said with a laugh, she used to have time to do aerobics class.

Bridget used to run 6.5 miles a day. She has also had catering experience and brings a wealth of cookie recipes to the business; but her bent is for healthy, organic, whole wheat recipes. Together they strike a very nice balance between decadence and ambition. For those looking for a low-fat, no-sugar breakfast, after a long morning bike ride, (or a walk across the street) there are the chewy, nutty, all-organic sourdough raisin rolls, made with fermented raisins, regular raisins and whole wheat flour.

There are also buttermilk scones, whole wheat date nut scones, bran muffins, pumpkin muffins, banana poppyseed muffins, coffee cake, lemon bars, and brownies. The selection of cookies runs from chocolate chip to Swedish Toralfas. Loaves of whole wheat and sourdough French bread are made on weekends.

Everywhere are subtle cow graphics, such as the black and white tiling on the floor of the bakery. More challenging to decipher is the graphic on their business card and sign, which at first appears to be a Rorschach ink-blot test, but turns out to be a cow hide. Nevertheless, their name upholds the integrity of a town with a noon moo; it's a name nobody's going to forget, and their mouth-watering baked goods are equally memorable, not heavy nor at all cow-like. Here is one of their muffin recipes:

Banana Poppyseed Muffins

Ingredients:

Yields 16 muffins
1 stick (4 oz.) unsalted butter
3/4 c. chopped walnuts
2 large bananas, mashed
1 cup buttermilk
3/4 cup light brown sugar
2 eggs
1-2/3 cup cake flour
1 Tbsp. baking powder
2 tsp. poppyseeds
1 tsp. baking soda
1/2 tsp. salt
1 Tbsp. sugar
1/3 tsp ground cinnamon

Method:

Melt butter over moderate heat until slightly browned. Set aside to cool slightly. Toast walnuts lightly. Whisk together butter, bananas, buttermilk, brown sugar, and eggs. Stir together flour, baking powder, poppyseeds, baking soda and salt. Stir dry ingredients into banana mixture. Fold in walnuts. Spoon into muffin cups. Stir together sugar and cinnamon and sprinkle a pinch on top of each muffin. Bake muffins in the upper third of the oven for 18 to 20 minutes until browned. Cool on rack.

ALAN SCOTT

For Alan Scott, oven-building and bread baking are a philosophy, a way of life. Those who have tasted his freshly baked bread are inevitably return customers. There's a satisfying, nourishing simplicity in the dark, whole grain texture of the round loaves, called *desem,* which he bakes in an outdoor oven in Tomales.

"I think it (bread baking) should be kept small and local. I am the small-oven man. The scale is so important. It's got to be a human scale. The best size for an oven is what one man can comfortably bake in one day," said Scott.

An Australian blacksmith and "man of many hats" by trade, Scott came to the US 10 years ago, looking for a spiritual direction. In West Marin he found the Blue Mountain Meditation Center, where the authors of *Laurel's Kitchen Cookbook* reside with their spiritual community. "They were in the process of writing the Bread Book and wanted a brick oven to bake traditional French country bread. So I helped design an original Finnish-style brick oven in 1981," explained Scott.

The project fascinated him, and launched him into research on the history and construction of ovens; Russian, German, and Finnish.

This evolved into his enlightened business, Ovencrafters, offering backyard oven plans and building instructions, custom design consulting, workshops, and a catalog of accessories. He also writes articles and bakes for the local community and his family. "It's an odd business," he noted. "I do a bit of everything."

"Everything **matters,"** he emphasized. "From how you make the bread to how you present it to the customer." He uses local, organically grown wheat, which is ground into flour the same day it's baked. "The fragrance of freshly ground wheat is delightful," he said. "They're all different.

"Hand kneading is important — to have physical contact with the dough. It's also important to use the purest spring water, and that the bread be baked in clear heat — no gas fumes. Finally, the passing on of the bread to my customers."

"It might sound corny, but love is a primary ingredient in good nutrition. It brings us back to scale: you can't love a million loaves of bread."

"I can't possibly give you the whole recipe for Desem bread," Alan explained, "It is 25 pages long, and takes two weeks to do... But I invite you to come to see the bread making operation. We get up at 4 a.m. on Thursday and Friday mornings." A friend and I took Alan up on this offer. We agreed that the whole recipe is complicated, but that those dyed-in-the-wool bread makers might appreciate the recipe for the sourdough starter used to make this very special bread. (Desem is Flemish for "starter")

Desem Sourdough Starter

Ingredients:

10 lb. sack of organic whole wheat flour (to surround the desem)
7-10 cups coarse stone-ground flour to go into the desem (can be part of the 10 lbs.)
pure unchlorinated spring water (not distilled)

Method:

1. Mix two cups of flour with 1/2 cup water to make a baseball-sized ball of stiff dough, adding more water if necessary. Knead it a few minutes, make it smooth and round and bury that ball in the sack of flour. Find a place that is consistently 50-55 degrees, like a cellar, and leave it for 48 hours.

2. Dig out the dough ball, and cut away the dry crust, discarding it, so you have about half left. With clean hands, slowly work in 1/4 cup of water to soften. Knead in one cup of flour and add needed water to make it the original stiffness. Bury it again in the flour, for 24 hours.

3. Repeat yesterday's procedure. It should have slight fragrance of fermentation this time. If not, add more water than before.

4. Repeat the procedure, burying again for 24 hours.

5. On the next day, instead of discarding half the desem, soften the whole ball with 1/3 cup water. Add 1 cup flour. Knead in more water if needed to get the stiff consistency. This time, store the ball in a closed, nonmetal container, like a glazed crock, or glass or plastic container. (If it's glass, make sure it's not airtight.) Or, Alan says, wrap it in a cloth. Leave for one day in the refrigerator.

6. Soften entire desem with 1/3 cup water and add 1 cup flour to it. Adjust consistency until dough is medum stiff. Knead it for 10 minutes. Cut into 4 parts. Store one part in the original container and return to refrigerator. Combine other three and leave to ripen 24 hours at room temperature (65 degrees), to use as your starter for sourdough bread making. You will need to use 25 percent starter to dough used in baking bread.

The desem will not have reached full strength for another week or two, with "feedings" every 2-3 days, but you can begin to use it now, allowing for longer rising time. It will keep in the refrigerator for three months.

LANNY PINOLA

The tour of Miwok Village, known as Kule Loklo, is well worth the drive up Highway One past Olema to the Bear Valley Visitor Center. The tour of Kule Loklo takes an hour and allows you to imagine how the Miwok Indians in this area must have lived. As our group ambled up the path, we stopped to listen to the wealth of information offered by our guide and native Miwok Lanny Pinola. "They lived high on the hog then, as Marinites do now," he noted with a grin. "They had abundant supplies of food — fish, shellfish, deer, elk, berries and nuts."

Sadly, we learned that a population of 3,000 Miwoks dwindled to 300 in only 60 years, with the arrival of the Spanish. Those who acquiesced to their Spanish captors were forced into slave labor in missions in San Rafael. Those who didn't met a worse fate. We learned of the disappearance of the condor, the coyote and the black bear, which once roamed these lands.

We learned of herbal remedies and lore: women were tattooed on their chins with sharp sticks of poison oak dipped in berry juice, to distinguish their tribe. When the Red Elderberry berries become bright red, the shellfish in the ocean become toxic. (We now quarantine shellfish during the summer.) Eucalyptus buds, boiled in water are a sure-fire remedy for menstrual cramps. The California Bay Laurel leaves

are a potent insect repellant, cold remedy, and when rubbed over the bodies of Miwok hunters, a disguise of human scent when hunting.

Closest to Pinola's heart is the ceremonial building and sweat lodge, or Lamma. "How many of you have never gotten angry at a person in your life?" he asked the group. No hands. "Well, since no one among the thousands of people I have taken through here can say they haven't been angry, you can imagine the Miwoks got angry, too. But in Miwok days, you could not enter the sweat lodge if you were angry at someone. This building is very sacred. So we have a ritual that we do to cleanse our spirits before entering. We place our right hand up, like so, and turn two times counterclockwise before entry." Each person completed the ritual and ducked down the low entry into the semi-dark earthiness of the lodge. It was good to be down there. No one talked. Even the kids were still. It was a rich, hands-on cultural experience.

The Miwoks ate vegetables during the summer, mostly watercress, miner's lettuce, turnip greens and clover. But the mainstay of their diet was the acorn. One dedicated volunteer, Sylvia Thalman, patiently explained how to make acorn mush, the Miwok way. Here is her recipe:

Kule Loklo Acorn Mush

Ingredients:

Tan Oak acorns, a basket full
water
salt & pepper to taste
sweetener, to taste
butter

Method:

First, harvest Tan Oak acorns in October. Shell the acorns, discard wormy ones. Dry them in the sun, taking the paper skin off. They'll be like big bumpy peanuts.

Then grind them in a mortar and pestle until as fine as cake flour. Place flour in a cheesecloth and rinse flour, letting water drip through it all night long, leaching the bitterness from them.

In a pot (the Indians used water-tight baskets) place 1 cup of flour and 3 cups water. Bring mush to boil quickly. It thickens like oatmeal. (The Indians threw clean hot rocks [basalt] right into the mush to heat it directly.)

The result is a bland, but filling, nutritional pudding, good with butter, salt and pepper, or sweetener, if desired.

SALADS & DRESSINGS

CANDACE WYATT

After wondering for 18 years, Candace Wyatt of Bolinas made a phone call that put her mind to rest. She called the adoptive parents of the son she gave up 18 years ago.

"It was a relief to know that he is alive, healthy and has a loving home," she said. "I've spent all these years hoping and praying, unable to forget. The adoption agency tells you you'll forget, but you don't. I felt I should honor his first 18 years with his family, but then I would begin searching for him."

When her son turned 18, Candace still had one more semester to complete her degree in Environmental Education at New College, but she joined a Birth Parents Group which met monthly. "For six months I gave it a lot of thought," she explained. "I asked myself, 'Does it really feel right?' I read books, talked to other adoptees and adoptive parents, and learned all I could about both sides of the issue.

"I was ready to search on Sept. 16. He was still in my mind (and on agency records) "Baby Boy Wyatt." I [mentally] named him William Patrick Wyatt. And he grew up."

The search was like a detective story, tracing clues, discarding false leads. A doctor who befriended her in the hospital at the time of the birth generously offered to pay her airfare and put her up in his home in Washington, DC, where she would begin her search. Friends offered both financial and professional assistance.

One clue in the search was the adoptive mother's PhD in Geology from UC Berkeley.

Wyatt started there, since women in that department were rare. A call to a friend in Berkeley who did a little research given this information and the approximate dates, revealed the mother's maiden name. From there she went to marriage records, and found the father's last name. Now she needed an address. A guess as to the location of the family, and some research in public records at the Library of Congress and she soon had an address. "It was incredibly easy," she said. But then came the phone call.

"There was no way to prepare the family for my call," Wyatt said sympathetically. "But I expected and was prepared for their disbelief and distrust. After many questions: "What do you want?" "How did you find us?" "What kind of person are you?" they admitted that though they had prepared themselves intellectually for the call, they were not emotionally ready. They were very upset. Adoptive parents often feel the child will want to go away with the birth parent, but it really only affirms for the child what they've gotten from their adoptive family. It releases them from the mystery about their real parents."

Six-foot-one, healthy, and a lover of physics, math and philosophy like the rest of her family, Candace has joyfully reunited with her son and his family. They have visited one another's towns and continue to stay in touch.

Candace is a salad lover, particularly a Caesar salad lover. She often prepares this recipe:

Candace's Caesar Salad

Ingredients:

1 clove garlic, peeled and minced
1/2 cup olive oil
1 cup cubed French bread
2 heads romaine lettuce
one handful Mesclun lettuce mix
1-1/2 tsp. salt
1/4 tsp. dry mustard
black pepper, grated
5 filets of anchovy, mashed to a paste
Few drops Worcestershire sauce
3 Tbsp. wine vinegar
1 egg
juice of 1 lemon
2-3 Tbsp. grated Parmesan cheese

Method:

Put garlic clove in olive oil and allow to sit for 24 hours. In 2 tablespoons of this flavorful oil, sauté bread cubes, until browned. Set aside.

Wash and dry lettuce well. Tear into 2-inch lengths, and place with Mesclun mix in a salad bowl. Sprinkle salt, dry mustard, black pepper, anchovies and Worcestershire sauce. Add vinegar and the remaining 6 Tbsp. garlic oil.

Simmer egg in boiling water for 1 to 1-1/2 minutes or use raw. Drop egg from shell onto ingredients in salad bowl. Squeeze lemon juice over the egg. Add toasted croutons and sprinkle on Parmesan cheese. Toss entire mixture well. Serve at once.

MERYL EVENS

Say "aerobics" and images of sweaty, panting, arm-flailing bodies in a steamy gymnasium come to mind. But, Meryl Evens, aerobics instructor at the Dance Palace in Point Reyes Station, explained how aerobic workouts have changed, becoming safer and more effective, with less flailing.

The idea of aerobics, she reminds us, is to increase the capacity of the heart to pump oxygen and blood to the body. As your heart becomes more efficient, it doesn't have to work so hard and comes back to normal more quickly after exercising — and you burn fat.

"So our goal is to get your heart rate up into the 'target range' — and keep it there for at least 25 minutes. You want to work between 65 to 80 percent of your maximum heart rate. Figure 220 minus your age equals your maximum heart rate, so your goal is to work at 65 percent of that figure. Ultimately your resting heart rate slows, which means you have to work harder to get your heart rate up, but the end result is a healthier heart," said Evens.

In the old days 12 minutes was a minimum aerobics set. Now they've found that the lower end of your range is more efficient at burning fat. It's more efficient to walk briskly for

30 minutes, than to run hard for 15 minutes. A good rule is: if you're out of breath, you're working too hard. So aerobics sets are 25 to 35 minutes long. Another change is from high-impact to low- or non-impact aerobics. In the low-impact, the large muscle groups, (thighs and upper arms) are worked closer to the ground and under much more control.

"In the old high-impact we'd be winging and swinging... but being under control takes a lot more energy, and you get your heart rate up faster. We don't start out with the long slow stretches anymore either," Evens said. "It's hard to stretch a cold muscle. So the warm-up is faster paced and shorter, with stretching at the end of the aerobic set."

There's a lot to learn. Instructors in one certification program undergo a three-year practicum and take a comprehensive exam like an SAT. They learn muscle groups and exercises which work each muscle. They learn how to count music, choreograph and memorize routines, as well as take pulse rates, and know what to do in emergencies. Because of this training, there are many fewer injuries, Evens said.

Here's a delicious low-fat recipe from Meryl Evens:

Wilted Cabbage Salad

Ingredients:

1 medium red cabbage, thinly sliced
1 medium onion coarsely chopped
2 large cloves minced garlic
3/4 cup cooked peas (optional)
1-1/2 tsp. caraway seed
1 tsp. oregano
2-3 Tbsp. balsamic vinegar
1 Tbsp. olive oil
1/4 cup toasted walnut pieces
Goat cheese, crumbled

Method:

Sauté seeds, oregano, onions and garlic in olive oil. Add cabbage and stir until wilted. Season with pepper. Toss in peas, goat cheese, walnuts. Sprinkle balsamic vinegar over top. Serve immediately. Serves 4.

Robert Hall

Under stately shade trees, at his home in Tomales, Robert Hall, MD, greeted me one quiet afternoon. The roomy, Victorian-style houses serve as Hall's psychotherapy clinic offices, as well as the base of operations for the Lomi School, which has been operating now for 20 years.

The Lomi School operates in three parts: there is the open-to-the-public Lomi County Clinic in Santa Rosa, a Lomi Bodywork training school at a nearby ranch, directed by Richard Heckler, and two schools in Europe, one in Italy and one in Austria, which Hall oversees.

The European Lomi School trains psychotherapists in somatic (mind-body) skills, combining academic study (classical Western psychology) with practical and individualized training in verbal and body-oriented psychotherapy.

"We train by doing," explained Hall. "It's a hands-on approach, addressing the student's own personal issues, which may either interfere or enhance his or her effectiveness as a psychotherapist."

In 1968, Hall held a position in the Army as Chief of the Department of Neuro-Psychiatry in Fort Knox, Kentucky. When he met Fritz Perls, the father of Gestalt Therapy, he shortly thereafter resigned from his Army post and moved with his wife and three children to Esalen. "It was like going from IBM to Disneyland," he said. "We lived in a log cabin in a forest in Big Sur."

Hall studied with Perls, Ida Rolf and became friends with Richard and Catherine Heckler. The foursome of Halls and Hecklers traveled to India together to study with a spiritual master, and with Randolph Stone, the founder of Polarity Therapy

(then the master's personal physician).

"We began working, combining our varied experience. My interest was in Gestalt and rolfing. Richard brought aikido and yoga. Allysa, my wife, was working with breath. And Catherine was a dancer. We were all meditators. So, we began to work on a program with the idea of integrating the Western psychological disciplines with traditional Eastern practices," said Hall. "The first workshop was held in Hana, Maui, in 1970 and evolved into the Lomi School. It's a long convoluted history, but basically we've been training ever since then."

"Basically, I am a teacher," said Hall. "The doing of the teacher-student relationship *is* the training. The personal growth is about how you work out that relationship. You begin with an unrealistic view of the teacher. Then realize that even the teacher is flawed, and then come to accept him with love. My students let me know about my shortcomings quickly." He paused and smiled. "I try to live a quality life...."

"What's a quality life?" He sighed. How about a quality day? Pause. "Okay, I would wake up happy," he began. "Then spend an hour in meditation and an hour of exercise. I would enjoy a leisurely breakfast, and then begin five or six hours of work I am happy doing. In the evening friends would come over for a dinner of healthy food and wine and an evening of comradeship."

"My friends would find this hilarious (giving out a recipe)," mused Hall. "I am notoriously inept in the kitchen — on purpose. I like people to cook for me. But I do have a recipe, and it's real good."

Robert K. Hall's Famous Sprout Salad

Ingredients:

lentil and fenugreek seeds
1 carton of cottage cheese
chopped scallions
tomato wedges
avocado slices
2-3 Tbsp. olive oil
a sprinkle of balsamic vinegar
dash of toasted sesame oil
dash of tamari (to taste)

Method:

First, sprout the lentil and fenugreek seeds in a jar in a cupboard, rinsing twice a day, for four days, or until they look like they're big enough to eat.

Mix olive oil, vinegar, sesame oil and tamari together in a jar. Then assemble the ingredients together to taste, pouring on the dressing and serve on lettuce.

DOUG PERRIN

Bolinas Peace Cafe celebrated its third birthday of dinners and consciousness-raising programs organized by the collective efforts of Doug Perrin, Jenny Ulrich, Elizabeth Sapani, and Roger Hurt this year.

On the second Friday night of each month, the Bolinas Community Center is transformed into a cafe, complete with checked tablecloths, candles, waitresses arriving promptly with steaming bowls of soup, salad and bread. It's good food and even better for the noble cause it represents.

The idea of doing a "peace cafe" originally arose from the need to develop a sound funding base for Condega, Bolinas's sister city in Nicaragua. Elizabeth Sapani came up with the idea of the café format, and they launched their first cafe at the Bolinas Public Utility District building on a Thursday night. They served Nicaraguan "comida tipica" — your basic rice, beans and tortillas. It was a success, raising more than $400 for the effort.

"We've gotten tremendous support from the community," Doug Perrin explained in his raspy, bass voice. "Warren Weber supplies us with salad lettuce, Jim Anderson creates a lovely poster each month, Dave Sobel supplies bread; Don Murch supplies us veggies, just to name a few folks. Lots of folks just come down and pitch in."

The program each month is always political. Except for four benefits for Condega a year, the program is open to other groups who need sup-port. "We haven't tried to avoid controversy," added Perrin, which is precisely why the programs are so interesting. Some of the evening presentations have included speaker Brian Wilson, Wavy Gravy, Vietnam Vets, Guatemalan Relief, El Salvadoran Relief, Honduran Relief, San Francisco Homeless, Earth First and the Palestinian Rights Organization from San Francisco.

"We started with plastic and paper plates, but over the years we've scoured thrift shops and found enough all-ceramic plates, bowls, silverware and cloth napkins to serve 60-80 people. It's more work for us, but it's worth it to not be cutting down forests for the cause of peace," explained Perrin.

A Minnesotan by birth, Perrin joined the Signal Corps at age 17 during World War II to be trained as a Japanese interception operator. After the war he went on to graduate from the University of Minnesota and Macalester College. He then embarked on a career as a commercial radio announcer, worked for an ad agency, and later came to Marin and taught music to junior high schoolers.

"But about the time of the Vietnam rebellion in the late 60s, I quit teaching school and retired early," he said, smiling.

Perrin makes cole slaw each year for Bolinas's Labor Day Street Fair, and often for the Peace Cafe. Here is his recipe:

Peace Cafe Cole Slaw

Ingredients:

Salad:
4 cups white cabbage
1 cup red cabbage
2-3 red onions
2 grated carrots (for color)

Dressing:
1-2 cups mayonnaise (to taste)
1/3 cup honey
4 Tbsp. Dijon Mustard
1 Tbsp. caraway seeds

Method:

Slice cabbage and onions thinly with a knife. Grate carrots, and toss together with cabbage. Mix together dressing ingredients and pour onto cabbage mix. Chill and serve.

Black Bean Salad Deluxe
from Elizabeth Sapani

Ingredients:

Salad:
3 cups cooked black beans
1-1/2 cup chopped vegetables, including:
 tomatoes
celery
red and green pepper
red onion
corn
cilantro

Dressing:
1/3 cup lime juice
1/3 cup orange juice
2/3 cup olive oil

Method:

Chop vegetables and mix together in a large bowl. Mix together in a jar, the lime juice, orange juice and olive oil. Pour dressing over mixture. Tosswell and serve.
The Peace Cafe often serves this salad with Tortilla Soup.

WARREN WEBER

Late drenching rains came as a surprise, so late in the Spring, turning West Marin soft, dewy and green again. Down on Gospel Flats in Bolinas, rows of thirsty baby greens, cabbages and lettuces soaked up the moisture from the warm loamy soil.

Warren Weber, owner and originator of Star Route Farms, and I walked along rows of leaves, at various stages of maturity — romaine, spinach, the deep-red radiccio, and the dark green Chinese spinach, tatsoi.

"In the 16 years we've been here we've probably grown every crop you can grow in this climate," explained Weber. "But in the last six years we've concentrated on salad greens and specialty crops like the Mesclun lettuce mix, edible flowers and herbs."

He filled my fist with tiny strawberries, and said "These are called 'fraises des bois.' We just sent off 18 pounds of these to a wedding in Pennsylvania."

Star Route Farms supplies Bay Area restaurants, markets and health food stores daily with fresh organic lettuces, greens and specialty fruits and vegetables. To name only a few, Chez Panisse, Stars, the Zuni Cafe and the Station House Cafe serve their fresh produce; and the Palace Market, Bolinas People's Store and Living Foods markets carry their stock as well.

Weber is a founding member and past president of California Certified Organic Farmers (CCOF) of Marin. At present he is on a committee to rewrite and upgrade the original bill spelling out what "organic" means and outlining procedures for transitional growers.

Originally, it was the "back to the land" movement in the 1960s that caught Weber's attention. He went to Cornell School of Agriculture for a degree in Farming Economics. A desire to teach at the college level took him back to school. He acquired a PhD in English Literature (Shakespeare) at UC Berkeley.

In 1974, he came out to Bolinas, bought the land on Gospel Flats next to the school and began farming. "We started with horses back then," he said with a smile as an electric cart quietly whizzed by us. "We were long hairs... We got a lot of free labor at first. Before us, this land was an artichoke farm, and way back in the 1800s, a race track went around the fields — the Gospel Flats Racetrack."

Today Weber's farm has expanded to 100 acres. Crop rotation and maintaining soil fertility are the mainstays of his organic pest-control system. He also uses "floating row covers" on seedlings — a gossamer-light veil to protect from bugs — safer soap on aphids, and occasionally torch-flames beds to destroy insect eggs. Each winter, cover crops such as vetch or bell beans fix nitrogen in the soil; soil is enriched with composted manure, lime, oyster shells and phosphorus.

"This is class one soil," Weber said looking out over the flats. "It's Blucher loam, four to six feet deep with gravel underneath."

Recipes using Weber's salad greens are as regular a daily regime as his evening run. Making a salad with them is as simple as scooping a handful of greens onto a plate. Here is one delicious version to try:

Star Route Farms Grilled Chicken Salad

Ingredients:

Per serving: 2 handfuls Star Route Farms mixed lettuces or baby greens. Choose from: Mesclun mix, frisée and escarole, hearts of Romaine; arugula.
1/2 chicken breast, skinned and boned
1 Tbsp. Dijon mustard
1/4 cup Balsamic vinegar
1 squeeze lemon juice
1/2 cup extra virgin olive oil
1/3 cup white wine or champagne vinegar

Method:

Wash and spin dry greens. Whisk together mustard, lemon juice, balsamic vinegar and olive oil. Combine 1/4 cup of this vinaigrette with wine or vinegar in a pan. Dunk chicken breasts to coat. Let stand 15 minutes to 1 hour. Preheat charcoal grill. Grill chicken breasts to desired doneness. Slice chicken and place on top of a bed of greens as individual servings. Drizzle with remaining vinaigrette. Serve with crusty bread.

JENNY ULRICH

Each month, Bolinas political activist Jenny Ulrich, with partner Doug Perrin and the Peace Cafe committee put on a vegetarian feed and political program, bringing up-to-the minute information on Third World and global injustices.

Ulrich was with the first group of West Marin residents that went to Bolinas' sister city Condega, Nicaragua, bringing precious medical supplies, and staying to help for a month.

Deeply rooted in Catholicism, Jenny came late to her political awareness. At age five, in Dayton, Ohio, she was brought into the Catholic church by her mother. After college she decided to go into a convent.

"I just wasn't happy," she said. "I was lonely. But I wasn't piously religious. I liked to play sports and dance. My friends were blown away when I decided to go." She spent seven years in a convent in San Antonio, Texas.

"As I began to study and teach in the next four years, I began to fall in love with people and have friendships with my 'brothers.' More and more, the vows I had taken didn't have meaning although I tried. My sisters saw my dilemma. I needed a man in my life, a partner, a daily presence. Finally I left the convent ... It was comparable to a divorce."

She went to study for a master's degree in Religious Education at Seattle University. In Seattle, Jenny learned about the "military-industrial complex, the Trident and the war machine."

She was married, and came with her husband to Bolinas, to work with Full Circle students.

The marriage didn't work out, but Jenny's political awareness grew in Bolinas. It was on her first trip to Nicaragua that she felt a reconnection with the church.

"In Nicaragua, everyone was Catholic. I worshipped often with the people; the priest in the village took us with him on sick calls or to celebrate Eucharist in mountain villages. We developed an important relationship with the priest and the people. I felt I needed to go back to my church and establish a sister church relationship."

Since then, Jenny has rejoined members of her faith at St. Mary Magdalene Church in Bolinas, with a new perspective. The priests in Bolinas and Condega now correspond; an annual brigade of 20 people goes down each February, to reconstruct houses and, this last time, to be official observers at municipal elections. A container is going this year, filled with tools — even a cement mixer.

Said Jenny, "When I became aware of environmental problems, I asked myself, 'Why aren't we as a church addressing this issue?' As a result, Father Decker and I wrote to other priests, and helped to organize the Christianity and Ecology conference for Earth Day 1990."

Here is a recipe from the Peace Cafe in Bolinas:

Carrot Salad Supreme

Ingredients:

Salad:
4 cups grated carrots
1/4 cup raisins or sweet red pepper
1/4 cup toasted walnuts or sesame seeds
4-5 green onions, chopped
2 cubed blocks of firm baked tofu

Dressing:
1/4 cup soy sauce
1/2 cup olive oil
1/2 cup rice wine vinegar
splash of sesame oil (to taste)

Method:

Salad:
  Combine carrots, raisins, toasted walnuts, green onions and tofu in a large bowl. Add dressing and toss gently.

Dressing:
  Combine olive oil, soy sauce, rice wine vinegar and sesame oil, and shake or stir vigorously. Toasted sesame oil is quite strong in flavor, so you will want to use it sparingly.

Sautéed Red Cabbage Salad
from Elizabeth Sapani

Ingredients:

1 chopped onion
1 small head red cabbage
oil for frying (not olive oil)
splash balsamic vinegar
1 ripe pear
1/2 cup toasted walnuts
crumbled blue or gorgonzola cheese

Method:

  Chop onion. Thinly slice one head of red cabbage. Chop one pear into small chunks. Toast the walnuts lightly in a baking dish in a low oven.
  In a deep skillet heat vegetable oil. Sauté onion in oil. As onion begins to turn transparant, add red cabbage. As cabbage begins to turn color, add balsamic vinegar and toss while still hot. Remove from heat.
  Add pear chunks, toasted walnuts and toss with cabbage. Crumble blue or gorgonzola on top. Serve warm.

KEITH HANSEN

In birding circles, word travels fast. When Keith Hansen of Bolinas spotted a rare, Russian Garganey duck, while on a walk through the sewer ponds, he knew that hordes of bird watchers would descend on the area to check out this rare, lost bird, if word got out. The same thing happened when a Siberian brown shrike showed up in Inverness Park earlier.

Bird watching, says Keith, is one of, if not *the* largest sport in the world — just after baseball. Hansen is one of the sport's enthusiastic participants as well as an accomplished bird and wildlife illustrator, having illustrated nine books, such as *Birds of Yosemite and East Slope,* and *California Wild Lands.* His next book will be for the Point Reyes Bird Observatory, a *Marin Breeding Bird Atlas,* by Dave Shuford. Hansen has so much illustration work lined up, he said, he's good for two to three years. "I'd rather draw birds than just about anything," he said with a grin. "I can't remember a day I haven't drawn, except to go out on a tour or something."

Hansen's enthusiasm for birds is infectious. From the deck of the home he caretakes on the Bolinas Lagoon he boasts the sighting of 227 species of birds. "We're tied for the highest number ever seen from the yard," he explained. "You see among birders there's yard lists and there's life lists. See that duck there? That's a Pelagic cormorant." He picked up his binoculars, handing them to me just as the duck slipped under the water, disappearing from view. Two sets of binoculars on stands stood next to us. "That's a black brant over there."

This passion for birds and art started in his family. Hansen says his mother encouraged all six kids in his family to draw and paint. When Hansen's older brother Rob did bird watching for a Boy Scout badge, Keith tagged along. "When I saw a cedar waxwing, it was all over. I couldn't believe how beautiful it was," said Hansen.

The family moved to Fresno, California, and big brother Rob began working at the Point Reyes Bird Observatory, learning to band birds from Bob Stewart. Twice a year the family would head to a far-away place called "Bolinas." It wasn't long before Hansen came back for longer periods of time for banding and bird counts.

Much of the research on birds takes place on the Farallone Islands, just off the coast of Point Reyes National Seashore. Hansen refers to the Farallones as magic. "It's refuge for thousands of sea lions and seals. Whales pass close by; one time we saw 55 migrating gray whales at one time. It's total serenity out there; but it is isolated and raw. The ocean is constantly pounding. You have to have a passion for what you are studying. There are two old houses built in the late 1800s. A diesel generator provides light, but there is only radio contact with land."

Hansen has earned a reputation for his guacamole, which he says he makes in huge batches with at least 10 avocados, testing as he goes. We cut the recipe in half for this occasion.

Keith Hansen's Guacamole

Ingredients:

5 avocados
1 pint sour cream
1-12-oz jar salsa (choose temperature)
2 large diced tomatoes
1 big diced onion
2 bell peppers, diced (green or yellow)
1/2 to 3/4 head garlic, diced
2 juiced lemons (have more on hand)
1 Tbsp. honey
1 bunch minced cilantro (if you like it)
salt to taste
pinch of cayenne

Method:

To open your avocados, stick with a knife, then cut it all around the long way. Then whack it to sink the knife to the pit and open the two halves. Quarter and 1/8th it. The peel will usually come off easily. Mash them with the sour cream. Add all the ingredients, leaving the lemon for last. Taste, adding more lemon if necessary. Serve with tortilla strips or your favorite chip. To keep it fresh, put one avocado pit in the dip.

COLLEEN MCDOUGALL

Colleen McDougall, of Olema, is part of a team of three psychologists directing the West Marin Community Outreach Project. For the past six years, she's been working toward her master's degree in psychology and now her MFCC (Marriage, Family, Child Counselor) license. While the part-time position won't make her rich, it comes just as she began to wonder if she would have to leave her home in the country for more lucrative pastures. She'd grown used to filling her lungs with fresh air on long walks in the woods and on the beach.

Colleen's job is to help people with addictions to drugs and alcohol, through education, counseling, and providing a confidential support system for kids, teens, adults and the Latino community in West Marin.

"I'm not sitting in an office waiting for people to reach me," said McDougall. On Thursdays, she "hits the streets" armed with condoms and information packets. She talks to street people. It's a hands-on exploration of what is actually going on in our community.

She is no stranger to the problems of alcohol and drug addiction. For the past three years she's worked with alcoholics and heroin addicts at the Marin Treatment Center. Though West Marin may look like paradise, there are those who are trapped in the cycle of substance abuse.

"People think heroin addiction is the worst addiction," said McDougall, "but any addiction is a problem if it's causing problems in your life.

The major problems are alcohol and marijuana in West Marin. Ninety-seven percent of alcoholics are functioning — have jobs, families and relationships. They're people you know well. Only one to three percent are the skidrow type of alcoholic."

"If you're wondering whether you're having a problem with drugs or alcohol, try abstaining for three months," McDougall suggests. "Just notice what happens. Do you miss it? Have cravings? Are you irritable? Find it hard to relax? You might consider trying to find alternative methods of dealing with stress (take a walk or hike, gardening, dancing, taking a bath, getting a massage, or meditating). It'll be different for everyone, but it's important to do something that revitalizes and makes you feel good. And, if you can't do it on your own, then seek the help of a 12-step program, or counseling, or both."

Eating lots of salad greens is a tasty way to get healthy. And the dressing makes the difference. Karin Wikstrom is the originator of this salad dressing. A Bolinas resident and artist, she always brought to potlucks a colorful and impressive salad on a huge ceramic platter which she had designed and glazed herself. Surprises like almonds and pieces of fruit or flowers could be found in them. But it was the dressing that made it superior. It is rich and creamy, but doesn't smother the taste of the greens.

Also included is another of Colleen's favorite salads.

Karin's Incredibly Good Salad Dressing

Ingredients:

3/4 cup oil
1/4 cup vinegar
Splash of soy sauce
1 heaping Tbsp. mellow white miso
2-3 Tbsp. nutritional yeast
1 tsp. honey or brown sugar
Splash of water
garlic to taste
Optional:
mayonnaise
ketchup
mustard and lemon

Method:

Blend all ingredients together, until mixture becomes a creamy, light brown color. Adjust optional ingredients to taste and texture, adding tartness or thickeners if needed. Miso or soybean paste is a good, low-fat source of protein and can be purchased in the health food sections of grocery stores. It is, however, very salty, so don't add extra salt.

Curried Tempeh Rice Salad

Ingredients:

Rice salad:
2 cups cooked brown rice
tempeh square, cubed, sautéed
2-3 cloves sliced garlic
1 thinly sliced carrot
1/2 cup toasted almonds or cashews
1/2 cup currants
1 minced green onion

Dressing:
1/2 cup orange juice
1/4 cup balsamic vinegar
Dash dark toasted sesame oil
3/4 cup olive oil
2 Tbsp. tamari sauce
2-3 cloves grated garlic
2-3 Tbsp. grated ginger
1/4 tsp. cayenne pepper
1/2 tsp. cumin powder
1 tsp. favorite curry powder (or make own)

Method:

Rice salad:
   Cut tempeh square into small cubes. Sauté these cubes with garlic in butter or oil. When nice and crispy and brown, remove from pan and set aside. Toast almonds in oven on low heat. Let cool before mixing. Mix carrot, currants, green onion, cooled tempeh and almonds together in a large bowl.

Dressing:
   Combine orange juice, vinegar, sesame oil, olive oil, tamari, garlic, ginger and spices. Pour over rice mixture. Chill at least an hour.

Serve over fresh greens.

MARION WEBER

We're never ready or willing for big life changes. Death, life-threatening illness, or the ending of a relationship is almost always untimely. It's during these times we're most in need of safety and companionship.

The Healing Arts Center in Stinson Beach, created by Marion Weber, is a place that recognizes that need for safety during times of change. In a little building across from the firehouse on Highway 1, Marion has set up a shop carrying books, cassettes, and videos both for sale and as part of a lending library.

It's an extensive collection of books on self-healing, as well as gifts and cards. Outside is a small building called the "sand tray room." A deck affords a peaceful place next to the creek for conversation or reading.

"What sets this bookstore apart from other 'New Age bookstores,' " Marion explained, "is that this one has a focus: bringing together creativity and healing in a practicum. I wanted to create a place for people in transition to talk, read, or just connect. Because I've been an artist and have worked with cancer patients, I've seen how important it is to trust the intuitive process, especially when we feel lost or wounded."

To this end she created the sand-tray room. She has used sand trays with patients at the Commonweal Cancer Help Program for over three years. It's a two-foot by four-foot tray of sand in the center of a little room lined with shelves full of small figurines and tiny objects. The user symbolically smooths the sand, clearing the mind, allowing the subconscious mind to choose objects from the shelves, thus creating a picture, or scenario, in the sand. "It gives you a sense of where you are and might be going. It's a creative self-help thing," explained Marion.

Marion Weber's artistic career began at 16 when her mother gave her a set of paints for Christmas. She went on to Boston Museum School of Fine Arts, spending her senior year in Florence, Italy.

While raising her two daughters in Bolinas, she dropped her art for five years to farm. "It was a lot of work, farming," she recalled. "But then I began making tapestries. It was through that work I got more in touch with art as a healing force for myself."

Marion gives us this fresh and healthy recipe:

 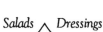

Marion's Mid-day Dressing

Ingredients:

2/3 cup safflower oil
1 tsp. soy sauce
1/3 cup organic lemon juice (2-3 lemons)
1/2 tsp. honey
2 cloves fresh garlic, minced
a sprinkle of cayenne pepper
1/2 tsp. peanut butter or Parmesan cheese (optional)
chopped fresh herbs: spearmint, chives, parsley
fresh organic greens

Method:

Mince garlic and fresh herbs until fine. Squeeze lemon juice from 2-3 lemons. Mix ingredients together in a jar and shake well. The peanut butter or Parmesan cheese gives the dressing a delicious hearty flavor.

Tear greens for salad by hand, adding chopped vegetables of your choice in a large wooden bowl. Pour dressing onto greens just before serving. Toss and serve.

SEAFOOD ENTRÉES

VIRGINIE BERGER

When a French woman offers to cook, especially Virginie Berger of Stinson Beach, I always accept. Dinner chez Virginie promises an evening-long experience in the artful seduction of the senses.

I found her in her cheery cottage kitchen, gently massaging an organic chicken. She welcomed me, gesturing with oily fingers. "I always massage these guys for a few minutes— under the wings, by the legs, and at the throat. Then, a little garlic under the skin in a few places, a little salt and pepper, and pop him in the oven. Voila, carry on."

She led me out to the back porch to pick some fresh chervil, roquette, and parsley from her potted herb garden. "I am a maniac about fresh organic produce. In France, my mother always took me to our garden to pick fresh vegetables for dinner. She was an excellent cook. You know, she is the one who inspired me. But French food at the beginning almost killed me. Mama's food was too rich. All this cream and butter. Nobody knew about diet back then. When I came to California I became a vegetarian.

"Then, wanting more adventure, I traveled to the tropics and made a living cooking aboard yachts. Once, on a cruise touring the Virgin Islands we had a terrible misfortune. We set sail with eight high-paying guests. Yes, I mean $3,000 a week they paid. It was very uptown — crystal and silver in the main salon for each meal. I was to be very well dressed. I was hired as the gourmet French cook.

"The ship was laden with a week's supply of fresh fruits and vegetables, fresh fish, meat, eggs, and of course wine and booze. It all must look very clean and elegant, and we must stow the food wherever we can in a very small galley.

"When you cook on a ship, everything moves. You have to work in a very small space and always at an angle. I made improvisation with wet cloths for anti-slip mats so things would not go whoosh off the shelf. This way I like to relax while we are underway. We cram food in every space, try to secure it tightly, but if not, suddenly you are on your hands and knees, catching avocados, tomatoes, apples. C'est catastrophe.

"I had finished serving the lunch this day and I go up on the deck. That day we took many tacks. My eggs were in a basket above the counter. The French *never* refrigerate their eggs, you know.

"Finally we drop the anchor, and I go below to fix the hors d'oeuvres. Everywhere was egg whites and yolks. I tell you it was horrible! And it had to be cleaned up in a jiffy, because if it dries, you cannot lift anything anymore from the floor."

Nevertheless, when invited to dinner chez Virginie, expect the best. She is extremely particular about her ingredients, using fresh, and organic produce when possible, and cold-pressed oils, raw cream and butter. She makes her own crème fraiche and her own mayonnaise (but of *course!*).

Here is a simple recipe Virginie created. "Ça jette," she says. (It *works.*)

Shrimp Allah
(Tunisian prawns in hot garlicky sauce. Serves one)

Ingredients:

6 medium prawns
1/2 cup white wine
1/4 cup heavy cream
a dollop of Harissa*
brown and wild rice

Method:

Begin cooking your rice. When it is near done, begin the prawns.

Toss prawns (in the shell) into a dry frying pan, medium heat. Toss them on both sides until pink. Add white wine. Toss around for a short time. Remove prawns with slotted spoon, and, as soon as handleable, peel shells, leaving tail on.

Add heavy cream to the bubbling wine. On low heat, whisk. Add a dollop of Harissa,* continue whisking. Add prawns. Serve over a combination of brown and wild rice, or just wild rice.

*Harissa is a very hot garlic sauce from Tunisia, found in gourmet stores in a yellow tube. It's what they use in real couscous of Northern Africa. Contents: Red hot pimentoes, garlic, oriental spices, salt.

MICHAEL BRYANT

A Japanese-Irish chef in Inverness is cooking up an international East-West blend of tastes at Barnaby's By the Bay.

Soft-spoken Michael Bryant has loved to cook for 20 years. Born in Occidental, he began his career in the restaurant business at 12 years-old, as a dishwasher. By the age of 16 he was managing his own kitchen. From there he studied under notable European and Asian chefs in the art of Italian, French, Cajun, Chinese and Japanese cuisine, in the Bay Area, Los Angeles and Florida.

Bryant's mouth-watering special menu starts with appetizers like "Drunken Shrimp with Ginger, Scallions and Saki" and "Warm Brie with Tomato Coulis and Pesto" or "Szechuan Cold Noodles with Enoki Mushrooms and Duck Sausage."

Special entrées include seafood selections, such as the favorite Sautéed Sea Scallops with Lemon and Thyme Cream Sauce, or Sautéed Halibut with Salmon Mousse and Champagne sauce. "The pink color of the salmon mousse, flecked with green, inside a firm white fish is very pretty," said Bryant.

Thursday night's Chinese menu requires a trip into Chinatown for specialty items and spices. On one Wednesday, Bryant's run happened to fall on the day before Chinese New Year. "They were four deep at the meat market," he said, "but I learned how to get attention at the counter. You put the money in your hand and wave it in the air over the heads."

Bryant's creativity with food is evident everywhere, but his treatment of vegetables is particularly loving. "I am very fond of salads. They are the most expressive for presentation. You can do a lot and make beautiful things with the bounty of vegetables available. A very pretty one was our Prawn salad with Papaya and Avocado with Raspberry Yogurt Vinaigrette, and this week's Salad of Baby Local Lettuces, Smoked Chicken, Baby White Asparagus, Sweet Peppers, and Chevito with Japanese Tarragon Vinaigrette was also nice."

Here is a recipe of Michael Bryant's, and one of Barnaby's most popular seafood dishes:

Sea Scallops with Orange Tarragon Cream Sauce

Ingredients:

1/4 cup white wine
1/2 cup heavy cream
1 oz. orange juice
5 oz. fresh sea scallops
fresh tarragon
salt and pepper
sliver of orange peel

Method:

Place one finely sliced orange peel in sauce-pan with wine, cream, and orange juice. Simmer over low heat until reduced by half. When it starts to thicken, toss in scallops for a mere 3 minutes on low heat. Add a big pinch of fresh tarragon, and salt and pepper to taste. (Serves one)

CARL AND ANITA HENRY

A few years of single life in Bolinas, after ending a 17-year marriage, convinced Carl Henry he was still a marrying kind of guy. And there's more than one way to find a wife.

"I decided to try the import model," joked Henry, glancing fondly at his pretty Philippino wife, Anita.

He ran a two-inch, one-time-only ad in the Sunday *Manila Bulletin*, describing himself, his two sons and his heart's desire: a female companion and wife.

"From that one ad I got over 750 replies," he said. "I spent months poring over the letters, and writing back to the most interesting ones."

He narrowed it down to 12 women and began corresponding with them on a regular basis. Anita Ellis was one of them. After six months, he had narrowed it to three women and decided to go to the Philippines and meet them. His two boys' only request was, "Marry a woman who likes children."

Anita and Carl met July 2, 1985, and were married on July 8, 1985. But not before they went to meet her parents in the town of Guinan, where Anita had grown up.

Henry recalled the harrowing trip. "We rode a bus all day, then slept aboard the deck of a freighter that night. On the boat I asked her if she wanted to be Mrs. Henry."

"It was right in the jungle... very primitive. There was no telephone, no running water, no electricity and no doctor."

But together they found a Spanish church in the jungle and, enlisting the help of siblings and cousins, managed to put on a festive marriage ceremony and suckling pig feast, complete with dancing into the night.

Anita recalled her first impressions of America, "I was scared because I have no relatives here."

"She came from a city of 12 million (Manila) to a town (Bolinas) of 2,000," added Henry. "She must have thought we were going to the end of the world."

There were extreme temperature changes for her as well. "The first time we went to Stinson Beach, Anita came out of the water and said, 'My dear, what is wrong with the water? It's like an anaesthetic!'"

Now there is a fifth member of their family: William Matthew Henry. Anita is very happily married. She says Carl cooks all the breakfasts and about 50 percent of dinners.

"I'll tell you, he's a good husband. That's the truth. He is a good, responsible man," she said smiling broadly.

Here is a Philippine recipe from Anita Henry's kitchen:

Whole Sweet and Sour Fish

Ingredients:

1 whole firm white fish (use firm white fish)
oil for frying
1 white onion, chopped
2 Tbsp. fresh ginger, grated
3-4 green onions, chopped
1 Tbsp. vinegar
1 Tbsp. sugar
1 can tomato sauce
dash red pepper

Method:

Clean fish. In a fry pan, fry fish whole in a little oil, until skin is nicely browned on both sides. Set aside.

Arrange a platter with lettuce, quartered tomatoes, onions. Place fish on platter.

Fry together in oil until transparent: onions, ginger, green onions. Sprinkle in vinegar, sugar, and 1 can tomato sauce. Stir. For spicier sauce, add red pepper. Pour this mixture over fried fish. Decorate with round onions on top of the fish. Serve with rice.

PAUL McCANDLESS

Bolinas musician and composer Paul McCandless is probably best known for his soulful saxophone solos, especially with the band Oregon. But he's also a recognized virtuoso on almost the entire reed family of instruments. He has released his own album on the Windham Hill label called *Heresay*.

With an advance from Will Ackerman of Windham Hill, Paul was given complete artistic control in producing the new album.

"I spent the whole winter writing music," he said. "I guess you could say I was inspired and driven. I would wake up at 6 a.m. with music going on in my head, go into my studio and often not come out until 4 or 5 p.m. It involved making choices and standing by them — a lot of decisions."

To play his music "incredibly well" on his album, McCandless chose pianist Art Lande, bass player (of Pat Metheny's group) Steve Rodby, flutist Wally King, Keith Green on French horn, and percussionist Trilok Gertu, all of whom he had known and played with over the years. McCandless himself plays eight different instruments on the album: piccolo and soprano sax, oboe, English horn, bass and B-flat clarinet, lyricon and penny whistles.

McCandless's passion for music runs in his blood. His father and mother, grandparents (on both sides), and two sisters all are musicians. "There are pictures of me as a boy with my cowboy hat, holster, and trombone in hand," he said. "Musical instruments were my toys. My mother taught me sight singing and piano; my father, oboe. They made a point not to push me into music, but I never knew there was anything else. I practiced all the time. I'd practice sometimes until my mother'd freak out. I found peace and privacy in it. In high school I'd play saxophone after school in the kitchen until I saw my folks at the mailbox. Then I'd quickly put the sax under my bed, and play my classical oboe études as they came in the door.

"I always said that when I made it" I would move to California to someplace like Bolinas. Then I realized that moving to Bolinas *was* 'making it.' I love to be here, but I have to travel to make a living. This is a special time," he said. "I am establishing myself as a soloist."

Still, I recalled, McCandless had found time to blow his sax with an impromptu group of musicians for Bolinas's Labor Day benefit. "I love that part about living in Bolinas," he said. "There's so much music here. It's what I can give back to the town for fund raisers and celebrations."

"A good artist is a good cook," said Paul. His wife Robin agreed: "He's a fantastic cook," she said. "But it's jazz cooking... He never follows a recipe and it's never the same twice."

Here are three she captured before they eluded the memory:

Paul's Blue Note Oysters

Ingredients:

1 purple onion
fresh basil, chopped
olive oil
2-3 cloves garlic, minced
1/2 cup sweet red pepper, chopped
dash of white wine
black pepper and salt to taste
1 jar oysters
Parmesan cheese
your favorite pasta

Method:

Chop onion. Sauté onion in olive oil with chopped fresh basil. Add sliced garlic, sweet red pepper, white wine, black pepper and salt, cooking until onion is transparent. Add 1 jar of oysters, and cook for 5 minutes. Serve over spinach pasta; sprinkle with Parmesan cheese.

Paul's Champagne Scallops

Ingredients:

1 yellow onion
1-2 Tbsp. butter
1 green pepper
1 cup champagne
1 lb. scallops
2-3 Tbsp. Parmesan cheese

Method:

Finely chop onion. Sauté onion in butter in a skillet over low heat. Finely chop green pepper. Add to onions. Cook for a few minutes, then add scallops and champagne. Cover. When scallops are almost done, pour off liquid into a separate pan. Sprinkle remaining scallops liberally with parmesan cheese, crushed garlic and lemon juice. Place under broiler. With remaining liquid, boil down to make gravy. Serve over rice.

Raging Shrimp

Ingredients:

1 lb. shrimp, cooked
2 onions, chopped
red peppers, chopped finely
celery, chopped finely
1/2 cup salsa, heat to taste
2-3 cloves garlic, minced
2 Tbsp. Tamari
pine nuts, toasted in a dry frypan

Method:

Sauté onion in oil until transparent, adding peppers and celery after a couple of minutes. Add shrimp, salsa, garlic, tamari and serve over brown Basmati rice. Garnish with pine nuts.

JOSH CHURCHMAN

Bolinas's Josh Churchman, a commercial fisherman for more than 20 years, is asking questions about where salmon we eat comes from. His concern for the future of salmon fishing and for public awareness of ocean ecology has led him to question man's intervention and "improvements" upon nature.

"There are virtually no natural spawning areas left in California, which will come as a surprise to some folks," he said. "About 99 percent of King Salmon sold is hatchery spawned and released in river deltas, such as the San Joaquin and Sacramento.

"A few small Silver Salmon runs are left in the Russian River and Papermill Creek, but dams on most major rivers prevent wild King Salmon runs which need a larger river and spawning area," said Churchman. "Silver Salmon, cousin of the King Salmon, brings a much lower price than the King, even though the two look and taste almost identical."

"King Salmon are herded into cement hatcheries and artificially inseminated. Only eggs and sperm of fish eight to 10 pounds are released to reproduce, which means diversity of the gene pool is being bred out. They're raised there to six inches in length and trucked to the river deltas where they are released."

The practice of pen-raising of salmon is rapidly taking the place of wild salmon runs in places such as Oregon, Washington, Canada and New Zealand. "These fish are bred and raised in pens. The reason to do this is to raise a perfect eight-pound fish," said Churchman. "Restaurants prefer their consistent size — they make perfect 6-ounce filets. A 15-pound salmon is hard to cut into even servings.

"But salmon are, like cattle, prone to disease in the pens and one diseased fish can infect thousands overnight. Therefore they are fed antibiotics," Churchman said. "The cages are painted with growth retardant, containing toxic heavy metals, which have been found in the salmon flesh. Last year they banned a material called Tributal 10, because of high levels of tin in salmon grown in those pens.

"Most people love salmon, and it's good for you — but I encourage people to ask at restaurants if their salmon is pen-raised."

"Man is the real danger to the future of salmon in California. I want to protect ocean wildlife and let people know what is happening to the natural habitat of salmon and other fish. We may be seeing the demise of salmon trolling as we know it.... I don't want my kids to grow up hearing only stories of how it used to be," he vowed.

Here is the favorite salmon recipe of Josh's wife Joy Churchman. She says it is a welcome variation to barbecued salmon:

Salmon in Grape Leaves

Ingredients:

1 lb. boneless tail filet of salmon,
 cut in 1 inch chunks
1 jar grape leaves, cut in half
1/2 pint sour cream
dill, tarragon, or favorite spices
chunks of avocado
capers

Method:

Mix the avocado, spices, and capers into a small container of sour cream. Dip salmon chunks in sour cream mix. Fold in grape leaf packets. Sauté in oil, 2 minutes each side. Serve over rice. Each packet blends grapeleaf flavor, fish and sauce in one bite-sized explosion.

Barbecued Salmon with Hoisin Sauce

Ingredients:

3-4 thick salmon steaks
1/2 cup horseradish
3/4 cup Chinese "Hoisin" sauce
1/4 cup olive oil
2-3 Tbsp. melted butter

Method:

Note: Use only very thick (1-1/2 - 2 inch salmon steaks), so that you can turn the steaks on the grill several times. You may need only 1 steak for 2-3 people.
Mix "Hoisin" sauce with olive oil. Set aside. Spread both sides of salmon steaks with horseradish. Place on grill. Turn when browned. Brush on hoisin mixture on one side. Grill several minutes. Flip them over and paint second sides. Cover the grill each time. It will smoke. That's good. In the course of 15 minutes, you will flip the steaks maybe four times. When it is pink all the way to the bone, paint it with butter. Cover again. It will be sweet and crunchy on the outside and just done inside.

JACK SIEDMAN

A slower pace was attorney Jack Siedman's goal, after several years of law work in San Francisco. Today his West Marin civil law practice allows him to coach Little League in the spring, soccer in the fall, and schedule fishing outings when the fish are biting.

"When my two oldest children were growing up, I missed too much of their lives," said Siedman. "I wanted to work more at home; I was disenchanted with the city."

A motorcycle ride to Bolinas one afternoon with a friend was pivotal. "We rode into town and there were all these dogs lying in the road. Two cars were stopped in the road while the drivers were talking to each other. I said, 'Here's a place that runs at my pace.'"

So in 1977 he moved out to Bolinas.

Siedman set up his practice in a little cabin behind his house — a general civil practice including litigation, family law, contracts, and real estate. Only 10 percent of his work takes him "over the hill," leaving the bulk of his attention focused here.

The oldest of three children growing up in Los Angeles, Siedman recalled, whenever he'd argue someone said he'd make a good lawyer. "In the 7th Grade they wanted to know what you wanted to do in your life. I just wrote

down lawyer. I still didn't know what it was. In fact, I never really examined that decision until I was 28."

In his third year of law school, he got a job with the San Francisco Neighborhood Legal Assistance Foundation, in the Chinatown office [part of Johnson's War on Poverty in the 60s].

"It provided legal services for poor people in inner cities, and me with a way to apply my legal skills for a social good beyond making money. Mostly my clients were poor Chinese, elderly Italians and beatniks, left over from the Kerouac days. I got experience in all kinds of courts right away."

In Bolinas Jack, his new wife Mary and their two boys, Nate and Joe, found few physical programs for kids. So they rolled up their sleeves and created them. Jack started the first Bolinas Little League team. Mary and Jack put together the Track and Field Day, a successful all-school competition.

Jack's been on the Bolinas-Stinson school board for nine years, president for three. He is also Chairman of the Firehouse Park Committee, working on a recreation area for all ages.

But of all his avocations, Siedman says he is probably most fond of fishing.

How to Catch and Cook an Eel

Ingredients:

To catch him:

1 old fishing pole
small hook
small pieces of squid

To clean:

Sharp knife
wooden board
several nails
pair of pliers

To cook:

1/2 cup cider vinegar
sprinkle of tarragon
sprinkle of sage
black pepper
sesame seeds

Method:

To catch him:

Take an old fishing pole, remove the eyes and tie a small hook at the end of the pole and bait it with a piece of squid. On the reef, look for crevices or underwater ledges where eels like to hide. Stick the bait right at the opening of the crevice. If you get a crab, it'll grab on and hold. If you get an eel, it'll hit the bait and pull hard. Throw back anything under 16 inches. A good-sized eel yields two to three pounds of meat, since there are virtually no bones.

To clean:

Gut the eel same as a fish. Make a circular cut through skin around base of neck, and two cuts through skin full-length of eel down each side of spine. Nail the head to a board, (otherwise you'll never be able to hold on to it to skin it) and using a pair of pliers, start at the base of the head and pull skin off one side, then turn it over and pull skin off the other side. Then remove the head.

To cook:

Pour vinegar over eel. Sprinkle on tarragon, sage, pepper, and sesame seeds. Cook under a broiler for 3-4 minutes on each side, until meat comes loose with a fork.

JIM BARNES

Firefighter and third-generation Woodacre resident, Jim Barnes is the guy that flies into the heat of the fire to drop the red powdery fire retardant, saving lives, property and wildlife. He flies to fire locations throughout California, from Ukiah to Santa Barbara. It's long hours, (10 days on, one day off) and can be very dangerous work, but he loves it.

The sophisticated detection and response system is a web of communication and technology, run like the military. Most of us hope we never have to experience it.

"We operate most successfully in keeping small fires small," said Barnes. "It's called a 'quick attack concept.' First priority is human lives, of course, then structures, property and wild land."

Much of his work involves fires started by lightning (thousands), which are quickly extinguished. But often crews fighting larger fires request his help, as in a fire near the Yuba River. "A 200-foot wall of flames rose up the riverbank. Lying just ahead of the flames was this beautiful home. People were just getting in their car to leave. I dropped the retardant down in front of the home.

"When a fire reaches this magnitude, it's like a volcano," he said, "creating a convection column of superheated air, smoke and debris, which throws burning debris 2,000 feet in the air, ahead of the fire, starting more fires. It's an incredible sight."

With wind shifts, ground crews, that one minute were in a safe position, can become suddenly engulfed in flames. Barnes saved ground firefighters' lives four times this year, by dumping the retardant directly on them.

"The retardant is chemically simple, like fertilizer you'd use on a lawn. The red is a dye, so pilots can see it when it's dropped. It fades in four months. We try not to drop it on people or structures, but we'll drop it on the crew in a life-saving situation. It must be dropped in a concentrated form to be effective."

"One of the biggest dangers is due to flying too slowly and stalling the plane. We fly in at 75 to 100 feet. There's always the danger of low visibility, power lines, flying debris. We've lost 10 flyers in 10 years. My last fire last year was caused by a friend who crashed in an attempt to put out a lightning fire. No one knows why.

"A real concern is the inaccessible, expensive homes in the woods. In areas like Mt. Tam, brush burns as fast as the wind at 20,000 degrees in the center .... I've seen whole towns burn to the ground."

Oysters in Bordelaise Sauce

Ingredients:

(for 200 small oysters)
4 cubes butter
2 bundles chopped parsley
4 heads (not cloves) garlic
couple "slurps" white wine

Method:

While oysters are on barbecue, mince the garlic, and melt the butter in a saucepan, adding garlic and wine. Sprinkle in the parsley. When the oysters open slightly, pry them all the way open and spoon the butter mixture on them. Place the oyster-filled shell back on the barbecue and let it cook down in the shell. Serve hot, if your guests haven't already served themselves.

MARTY ROSENBLUM & BETSY AYERS

They're a match made in heaven and they know it. Marty Rosenblum, a rangy, Jewish New Yorker and Betsy Ayers, firey, energetic and Spanish/Filipino, are the creators of "Marty's Parties," a catering service located on Sir Francis Drake in Lagunitas.

Marty's Parties has wined and dined the likes of Carlos Santana, Herbie Hancock, Bill Graham, CBS Records, Grateful Dead ... even Delta Airlines, to name only a few. They've thrown parties at the Fillmore, "Gone With The Wind" parties, and weddings in the middle of the woods, where there's no kitchen at all.

As we sat in front of their shop in the afternoon sun, they took turns telling their story:

"We lived two blocks from Grandma," Rosenblum reminisced. "Every Sunday we'd go for dinner — turkey, steak, ham and apple pie — the works. For dessert we'd take butter pecan ice cream into the living room to watch Dick Clark's American Bandstand."

Rosenblum liked cooking so much he enrolled in the Hotel Restaurant School at San Francisco City College and upon graduating took a job cooking at the Marin Tennis Club, in San Rafael.

Ayers described her childhood home. "My folks would start dinner at 9 a.m. and have it done by 10 a.m. That's *a.m.* The house always smelled of garlic. Oriental breakfasts often consisted of prawns fried in garlic and garlic-fried rice ... or Cheerios.

"I'm an organizer, and I guess those skills came from my mother. I knew that after I graduated I wanted a paycheck. I took every business course, every home ec course I could find — I even repeated the cooking course."

Their stories merged in 1978, after Betsy'd had enough single life. They traveled through Europe together, with pots and pans and olive oil. "We wanted to cook as we went and shop in local markets," explained Ayers. "We traveled through England, Switzerland, Holland and Greece, cooking."

When they returned, they decided to cater together, working for catering companies in the Bay Area. Soon they became confident that they could cook, display and serve party menus that were more elegant and tasty than those they saw being served elsewhere. They made the break, and named their own catering business "Marty's Parties." "My name didn't rhyme," said Ayers with a smile.

"Catering is unloading and loading food," Ayers added. "People ask me why I'm not fat. I carry 50-pound bags of ice, 8-foot tables... I get lots of exercise."

Marty gives us this recipe, one of many in their collection.

Champagne Mustard Prawns

Ingredients:

2 tsp. minced shallots
1/2 cup olive oil
1 Tbsp minced fresh chives
2 lbs. large peeled deveined prawns
3/4 cup dry champagne
Juice of 1 lemon
1 Tbsp. butter
2 Tbsp. Mendocino mustard (hot, sweet)
fresh ground pepper

Method:

Heat olive oil in a large skillet. Add shallots, chives for 1 minute. Add prawns, sauté 30 seconds each side, until pink. Add champagne, bring to boil. Turn off heat, blend in butter, mustard, lemon juice. Sprinkle with fresh ground pepper. Serve over noodles or rice.

KAYOKO BIRD

At first glance, you'd think she was fresh out of college, but Kayoko Bird, high-spirited and ponytailed, has already had an impressive career as a painter both here in California and in her homeland of Japan.

Kayoko's family sent her to a two-year college in clothing and kimono design in Kobe, her hometown, and she studied with a master of traditional Japanese brush painting. But in a traditional Japanese family, there were not many career opportunities for women beyond that of housewife.

"They told me to forget about career," said Kayoko. "So I married a man, a salary man eight years older than I was. I was 20. It was a very big, expensive Shinto wedding ceremony."

But life as a housewife did not suit Kayoko. "The house was prison to me, every day the same. I lost 20 pounds in six months. I asked for a divorce. My husband didn't understand divorce; it was sin. But he finally agreed. I went home again to live."

A few years later, Kayoko was introduced to an American man, fluent in spoken and written Japanese, from California. "He asked me 'what do I want to do with my life?' I was shocked. This was an alien request to a Japanese girl. I said, 'I want to paint,' and he said, 'I'll support you.' "

They were married. Kayoko began to study with a Japanese oil painting master in the Western style and also began taking lessons on the *koto,* a 13-stringed musical instrument. She painted intensively. They moved to the Bay Area so her husband could finish his master's degree at UC Berkeley.

"I was getting the western idea by then," Kayoko said. "What a land, I thought — everybody getting what they want. I wanted to study painting more. I applied for scholarship to California College of Arts and Crafts (CCAC). My husband was surprised when they accepted me. I got four grants .... I gained energy in California. I became strong, and at school I was getting attention. I arranged a show in Kobe (in 1983) of my oil paintings. Five major newspapers wrote of my work. The next year, I showed in Fukuoka, Japan — a successful show also. Then my husband wanted a divorce. It was very hard. That was when I realized how important my friends were."

Remarried and settled now in Muir Woods, Kayoko continues to paint and show her work.

Kayoko offers us this inventive twist on a traditional tempura recipe.

Indonesian-style Japanese Tempura

Ingredients:

To dip: Use shrimp, firm fish (ling cod, snapper) or just vegetables, (broccoli, zucchini, asparagus, carrots)

Marinade:
1/2 cup soy sauce
1/2 cup sweet sake
1 tsp. minced garlic
1 tsp. minced ginger
1-2 minced green onions
a sprinkle of sugar

Batter:
1 egg
3/4 cup ice water
1 cup flour
safflower oil

Method:

Marinade:
   Mix together soy sauce, sweet sake, garlic, ginger, green onions and sugar. For fish, soak in mixture one hour or more. For vegetable tempura, add this mixture directly to batter.

Batter:
   Mix flour, egg and ice water with a fork until it looks smooth like pancake batter.

Deep fry:
   Heat safflower oil in a deep fry pan or wok. To test oil for heat: drop batter in. If ready, it sinks then pops out after 1 second. When ready, dunk vegetables or fish pieces into batter. Drop into hot oil until golden brown. Remove and drain on paper towels. Serve with squeezed lemon, with Japanese rice and miso soup.

KAREN HORTON

She strode through her kitchen, tall, blond, and unruffled by an afternoon of cooking, extended a warm handshake. "Something to drink?" she offered.

Karen Horton, cook and co-owner of the Stinson Beach Grill, and I took a seat at a small table in the cottage-style turquoise-and-pink dining area. To my surprise, she had spent the greater part of her career in the newspaper business.

She'd been a reporter for *The Sacramento Union,* where she met her writer-husband Tom. They have co-authored two guides, to Hawaii and Los Angeles, both published by Doubleday Press. The purchase of the Grill in 1986 began their their first venture in the restaurant business. They aren't looking back.

From court reporting to cooking? Karen smiled and said, "Isn't it nice that now we can change careers in midlife and go and do something different?"

"My husband Tom and I have always been restaurant goers, and I've always loved cooking. I can't resist the cookbook section of any bookstore. I still have my first cookbook which my roommate (a food editor) gave me—*Better Homes and Gardens.* It's dog-eared, but it's an old friend."

Her work as kitchen manager, she said, is different in that it never stops. "I was used to deadlines. I'd finish the story and be done. Here it never ends... There's so much to be done."

The menu of the Stinson Beach Grill reflects Karen's eclectic taste in food, everything from Sunday brunch cheese blintzes to Cajun swordfish to Indonesian lamb with peanut-coconut sauce.

"I love seafood, and there's so much available here," she enthused. "And I love pasta and Italian food. We'll have lobster or pesto sauce on linguini topped with grilled prawns.

Grill.

We always have fresh cheese, veal or spinach ravioli from North Beach, which is worth the hassle of finding a parking place to get."

The seafood at The Stinson Bar and Grill is excellent, but so are the more exotic dishes. I tried their Chicken Molé, for instance, served with a peach salsa, wild rice, and grilled chicken with chocolatey molé ladled on top. It was heavenly.

Here is a recipe from Karen Horton, and the Stinson Beach

Oyster-Stuffed Steelhead Trout

Ingredients:

1 bunch green onions, minced
1 carrot, diced
5 Tbsp. butter
2 cups cooked wild rice
18 small shucked, chopped oysters
1 egg, beaten
3 Tbsp. seasoned breadcrumbs
   (basil & oregano)
1/4 cup minced parsley
3 tsp. orange rind, grated
Salt and pepper to taste
6 cleaned whole trout, 8-10 oz. each
4 Tbsp. melted butter
2 Tbsp. fresh lemon juice

Method:

Sauté onions and carrots in melted butter until soft. Add in bowl to rice, oysters, egg, breadcrumbs, parsley and orange rind. Mix well. Add salt and pepper. Spoon filling inside each trout and fold closed. Place trout in buttered baking dish. Brush with melted butter and lemon mix. Bake at 400 degrees for 20 minutes, until skin is crispy and brown. Serves six with the following sauce.

Orange and Shallot Butter Sauce

Ingredients:

2 Tbsp. minced shallots
2 Tbsp. white wine vinegar
1/2 cup white wine
1/4 tsp. salt
1/8 white pepper
Juice from one orange
1/2 lb. butter, in small pieces

Method:

Cook shallots, wine vinegar, wine, salt, pepper and orange juice in saucepan to boil. Let simmer briskly for a few minutes. After removing saucepan from heat, add butter and mix until butter melts. Spoon over each trout.

MICHAEL WATCHORN AND JOHN FINGER

These two young oystermen, Michael Watchorn and John Finger, are the originators of the successful Hog Island Oyster Company, located on Tomales Bay, along Highway 1 in Marshall. Their headquarters, now in the old general store building, is soon to be moved next door to the historic Marshall Tavern building.

That's good news for oyster lovers. The new tavern will house a 60-to-100-seat restaurant over-looking the bay, serving up Hog Island shellfish, wines of Sonoma County, and fresh fish and crab from Tomales Bay. A small wharf will hold seawater live-tanks for the sale of oysters to the public.

The prime season for oyster-eating is the winter months, from November through April. Tomales Bay, a narrow, 14-mile-long body of water, with the Point Reyes National Seashore on one side, provides a near-perfect set of conditions for cultivating oysters, flushing itself on each tide, and being replenished with clean, fresh, ocean water and just the right proportion of fresh water from Walker Creek.

The most popular oyster is the Hog Island Sweetwater, a plump oyster with a fluted shell in shades of cream, purple and black. They also cultivate the

Kumamoto, a round, buttery oyster in a deeply cupped shell, and the French Belon, known to some as the European flat oyster.

Hog Island oysters are now distributed to some of the finest restaurants in the world — to tables in New York, Chicago, Washington, DC, and as far away as Singapore and Hong Kong. Michael showed me an impressive glass-engraved trophy — the California "Wine and Food Achievement Award," which Watchorn and Finger won for animal husbandry.

Hog Island has tripled its sales each year since the business got rolling in 1984. "As long as the bay stays clean, our business should thrive," said Watchorn. "The seafood trend hasn't dipped in 20 years."

Making sure the bay stays clean has become a real concern to oystermen and shellfisherman all around the bay. "We formed the Tomales Bay Shellfish Growers Association to officially put down our stance," said Finger. "When I started this business, political issues were the furthest thing from my mind. But we've had to become vocal on environmental issues," added Watchorn.

Here are two recipes from two Hog Island oystermen for sauce to swill down with your chilled oysters on the halfshell.

Hogwash

Ingredients:

1 pint rice vinegar (1/2 seasoned, 1/2 plain)
2 medium shallots, finely chopped
1 large Jalapeño pepper, finely chopped
  or serrano chili pepper to make it hotter
juice of 2 limes
1 bunch of cilantro, coarsely chopped

Method:

Combine and chill for one hour. Serve in a bowl on crushed ice, next to your plate of oysters on the half shell.

Mignonette (Sauce)

Ingredients:

1 pint Balsamic vinegar
1 cup dry sherry
4 medium shallots, finely chopped

Method:

Combine and chill for one hour. Serve in a small bowl next to a plate full of raw oysters on the half shell.

MARGOT PATTERSON DOSS

The Bay Area's best-known walker, Margot Patterson Doss, moved from her home of 30 years in San Francisco's Russian Hill to Bolinas's Horseshoe Hill. A nasty broken ankle suffered just before the move hardly broke her stride and certainly not her spirit.

For 28 years, Doss's column "Bay Area at Your Feet" in the Punch section of Sunday's *Chronicle-Examiner* guided pedestrians over urban and coastal paths and served as her forum as an environmentalist.

In her famous red-plaid cape, she has walked with television cameras for over seven years on *Evening Magazine* with Jan Yanehiro and Richard Hart. She was instrumental in the formation of the Golden Gate National Recreation Area (GGNRA), and now serves on the Citizen's Advisory Commission to GGNRA and the National Seashore.

Her column has resulted in the publication of 11 books. Among them are *Bay Area At Your Feet, San Francisco At Your Feet*, and *A Walker's Yearbook*.

Her walks have by no means been limited to the Bay Area. Doss has walked and written about adventures in Samoa (where she and her husband John Doss, MD, lived for two years because of his work with

the World Health Organization), Japan, Thailand, China, India, Britain, Mexico and South America, to name a few places. She regularly contributed travel stories to *Venture Magazine, Oceans, Asu Travel Guide, Pacfic Discovery* and others.

"This is the original writer of walks," she said handing me a copy of Pausania's *Guide to Greece*, a detailed account of the cities of Greece written 2,000 years ago.

An accidental journalist, Doss's first choice was a career in paleontology. Unfortunately few schools offered doctorate programs in the field for women. She wrote for *The Bloomington* (Illinois) *Pantagraph*. It was publisher Adelaid Stevenson who taught her to write, she recalled. "He was subtle and witty, with a gift for seeing a situation in its totality. I was sent on assignment to cover an event at the Unitarian Church where young people were speaking. Later, back at the office, he inquired as to what I thought of the meeting. I offered my story which he read and thoughtfully added, 'If I may, please, I would have one addition?' He wrote, 'Youth took the witness stand tonight in its own defense.' That lead sentence turned the story into a feature."

Kokoda (Raw fish in coconut cream)

Ingredients:

1 lb. scallops
1 cup lime juice
1 cup coconut cream
2 inch piece fresh ginger
3 minced jalapeño peppers
1 minced onion (chives or green)
watercress or cilantro leaves minced
with cucumber

Method:

Soak fish overnight in lime juice. Then drain off 1/2 juice. Add coconut cream, chili, ginger and peppers. Coconut cream can be purchased in a can in the foreign foods sections of most markets. It shouldn't be the sweetened kind, rather the plain, coconut milk. Let sit an hour. At last minute stir in watercress and cucumbers. Serve on bed of lettuce or a banana leaf.

Steamed White Fish

Ingredients:

1 lb. firm white fish (3-4 filets)
4 sheets Nori seaweed
1/4 cup Wasabi powder (Japanese horseradish)

Method:

Prepare a large steamer pot, and begin heating the water to a boil.
Mix Wasabi powder with drops of water until it becomes a paste. Brush each side of fish filets with Wasabi. Fold flattened filets into a square shape. Toast Nori seaweed sheets, by passing them over an open flame. Run water over the sheet. Wrap up the fish in Nori seaweed sheets, like a package. Repeat with the other filets. Set in the steamer. Steam 6 minutes per inch. Average 12 minutes. Serve with rice, salad and the following dipping sauce, or refrigerate and serve thinly sliced on crackers.

Dipping Sauce

Ingredients:

1/4 cup sherry
2 Tbsp. light soy
grated daikon or radish
1 tsp. rice vinegar

Method:

Combine sherry and soy sauce. Grate daikon radish into mixture. Add vinegar. Serve in separate dipping dishes with the seaweed-steamed fish.

RUBY LEE

Ruby Lee's forceful, lifelike images draw comments like, "Wonderful ... and so strong," from folks who see her work, which has been exhibited in the Bolinas Post Office and in her own gallery, in downtown Bolinas.

Ruby Lee, with her dark hair and eyes, sat cross-legged on a large pillow, looking as Indian as the portrait of Native American leader Dennis Banks above her head. He faces the sky, eyes closed in a trance-like pose that is so realistic, it makes you hush to a whisper.

But Ruby Lee hasn't a drop of Indian blood in her veins. Her father, a Reuters journalist, is of Chinese and Viennese decent. Her mother, Japanese and English. She was born and raised in Asia, then England, Japan and Europe. Ms. Lee's grandfather, Long Tack Sam, was a stage magician who toured the world with Chinese acrobats.

Ruby Lee began painting and drawing when she was four. When she turned 17 she was enrolled in art school in London, but decided that wasn't for her. What she wanted was life experience and set off on trips to Spain, Greece, Israel, "all over Western Europe and the Middle East."

"Now I don't travel anymore," she added, "my paintings do." She has paintings in galleries in Romania, New York, Paris, Japan and Europe. She was commissioned by Prince Faisal of Saudi Arabia to do a portrait of the Crown Prince Abdullah on his Arabian horse. She showed me a copy of *Turtle Magazine*, which bore, on the cover, one of her paintings of Indians in the Run for Land and Life, a relay run across America from Onondaga Indian territory in upstate New York to San Francisco.

A big smiling face of Wavy Gravy, of the Grateful Dead is one of her most notable images. Ruby Lee said she met him in Point Reyes Station in 1985 at the Earth Festival. "Here was this big clown dressed in rainbow colors, putting on his white-face make-up. We started talking, and I was so inspired by his light — that I painted his portrait for his 50th birthday rock concert benefit."

Here is a recipe from Ruby Lee:

Ruby Lee's Prawns
with Broccoli, and Shitake Mushrooms

Ingredients:

1 lb. medium prawns, de-veined and peeled
3 cups broccoli tops
2 cups Shiitake mushrooms, cut into strips
1 clove garlic
1/2-inch square fresh ginger
4-5 shallots, diced
1 Tbsp. butter
Dash olive oil
1/4 cup tamari
1 tsp. arrowroot starch (available in health food stores)

Method:

Steam broccoli for 2 minutes; remove from heat. Blend arrowroot with small drops of water until it becomes a paste. Add more water to make 1/4 cup of liquid. Add 1/4 cup of tamari. Stir, and set aside.

In a frying pan, heat butter and oil. Sauté finely chopped ginger, garlic and shallots until shallots are clear. Add shrimps, turning frequently until pinky-peach color. Then stir in the broccoli and the shiitake mushrooms, cooking very fast, until broccoli turns brilliant green. Add tamari mixture. Stir as liquid thickens to a sauce. Serve over rice or noodles.

VEGETARIAN ENTRÉES

ARTHUR OKAMURA

Looking at the world the way Bolinas artist Arthur Okamura does, is a lot of fun. He's a painter, printmaker, teacher, magician, origamist, cook, athlete, and father. And he designed his large studio for the dual purpose of ping-pong and painting.

A professor at California College of Arts and Crafts (CCAC), Okamura teaches 50 new students each semester in painting, drawing and printmaking. His own paintings sell for upwards of $10,000.

To the under-10 set, he is a magician and he has published a book of magic tricks, which he wrote and illustrated, called *Magic Rabbit*.

Magic Rabbit is the result of years of collecting tricks. Arthur explained, "They aren't puzzles or 'hocus-pocus' but do-able things — physics — that actually happen. One trick is how to cut up a banana without removing the skin. I tested these tricks on people to see if they could do them."

Since he was a small child, Arthur has been facile with his hands; his job in his parents' San Francisco restaurant business was the not-so-simple task of butterflying shrimp, and making radish roses. (The secret of radish roses, says Arthur, is the ice water, which makes them expand as they soak.) He always wanted to be an artist. As a kid he was constantly drawing.

But within three months of Pearl Harbor's bombing, when Arthur was eight years old, the Okamura family found themselves incarcerated in a government relocation camp — a Japanese family in a suddenly hostile land. "It was terrifying," he said. "It was an awful feeling of guilt to be Japanese in America. We were in a camp in Colorado for four years. I remember going too close to the fence, once. The armed sentry in the tower ordered me away from the fence, looking down the barrel of a machine gun. But after two years, the guards went away."

"When I was 15, I wanted to be a magazine illustrator, a la Norman Rockwell," he said. "So I went to a commercial art school. Our family had moved to Chicago from the camp, where there was known to be less prejudice and more jobs. I worked for a silk-screen poster company. After 12 years with them, I was their main artist. But then I started to see modern art — Picasso and DeCooning. I resisted abstract art at first, but then realized I didn't want to do commercial art. I was excited by abstract painting."

"All the while, I was a quasi jock; I was on the track team. Later on I left painting to join the San Francisco Fencing Academy — a sport where it didn't matter that I was small. I'm still a jock," he said with a smile. "I play ping-pong eight hours a week."

As he spoke, he rolled up a paper tube of newspaper, then cut into its sides. Easing the paper inside out, he made a magnificent wand with spurs at regular intervals. Origami. Just for fun.

Arthur Okamura's Tempura

Ingredients:

Oil for frying
1 cup chicken stock
1 egg
1/2 cup corn starch
1/2 cup flour
onion
asparagus
artichoke hearts
sweet potato
carrots
bananas

Method:

Chop vegetables into bite-sized, manageable pieces. Keep them very cold, in the refrigerator.

Blend the stock, egg, starch, flour and salt, to taste. In deep pan, heat oil until batter explodes on contact.

Dunk ice cold vegetables into batter, and quickly into hot oil. Fry until golden brown. Remove, drain and serve hot with the following sauce.

Tempura Sauce

Ingredients:

1/2 cup mustard
1 Tbsp. soy sauce
1/2 cup ketchup

Method:

Blend mustard, soy sauce and ketchup together in a small bowl with a spoon. Makes a nice dip for tempura vegetables.

CINDY OHAMA & CAROL WHITMAN

The idea of an indigenous West Marin cookbook can be credited to Jane Boyd of Point Reyes Station, who first thought of it as a fun way to benefit the Dance Palace Building Fund, explained Cindy Ohama and Carol Whitman.

"I assumed she meant to benefit the West Marin Health Project," said Ohama. "So we started organizing. For quite a while we each had a different recipient in mind."

This little imperspicuity went unnoticed while they began to organize a game plan for putting such a cook book together, each enlisting more enthusiastic volunteers for their "mutual" project.

No matter. When they did finally discover each other's intentions, they quickly decided to make it a joint effort to benefit *both* the Dance Palace Fund and the West Marin Health Project. Besides, they agreed, it really is too big a job for each alone.

It wasn't hard, in this town, to find interested volunteers to help with a local cookbook. Everyone loves to eat. Everyone has a recipe they love to share. Well, almost everyone. A post office box was set up to receive recipes from community members, and recipe donation forms could be found around Point Reyes Station.

"These kinds of cookbooks sell very well. Since we're a tourist town, it's a perfect gift from the area for tourists to take home with them. It's also a great gift for out-of-town families of locals," said Carol Whitman, co-chairman of the project.

She was right. The cookbook, now published, is titled, *Home On the Range* — a large glossy-covered paperback, replete with local art work, and local cooks' recipes. It can be found locally in bookstores, at the Palace Market, and Toby's Feed Barn in Point Reyes Station. It has been a successful community fund-raising project, and a model for this book as well. Many of the contributors to the community cookbook, of course, can be found in these pages.

Here is a recipe from Carol Whitman's kitchen, from *Home On the Range.* "My son, given his choice of fare for his twelfth birthday, chose spinach lasagne!" said Whitman with amazement, "over hamburgers or pizza!"

We also included another recipe from *Home On the Range* from Cindy Ohama's kitchen, reprinted at her suggestion, since it is one of her foolproof favorites, Potato Cauliflower Curry.

Spinach Lasagne Swirls

Ingredients:

1 box lasagne noodles
large jar spaghetti sauce (or homemade)
1 pint ricotta cheese
1/2 cup Parmesan cheese
1 package frozen chopped spinach
dash nutmeg
salt, pepper to taste

Method:

Cook the spinach according to directions. Boil water for the noodles, cook. Mix cheeses, nutmeg, salt and pepper with cooked, drained spinach. Take each noodle, spread cheese mixture on the noodle, roll up and turn on end in baking dish. Cover with spaghetti sauce. Bake uncovered at 350 degrees for 20-30 minutes.

Potato Cauliflower Curry

Ingredients:

3 Tbsp. butter
1 Tbsp. turmeric
1 tsp. cumin
1 tsp. dried coriander
1/4 tsp. cayenne
1 good sized head cauliflower, coarsely chopped
6-7 medium potatoes, chopped
1 tsp. salt
1/2 tsp. black pepper
1 package frozen peas (or fresh)
fresh cilantro, chopped (optional)

Method:

In a heavy frying pan, melt butter, add spices, and stir until sizzling. Add 1/4 cup hot water and simmer for 1 minute.

Add to butter mixture and sauté for 10-15 minutes until well coated and hot.

Add to mixture, cover and cook over low heat, stirring occasionally until vegetables are done. Add water if necessary.

Keep mixture hot until five minutes before serving time. Add peas, cover and serve with chutney. Generally this is a side dish, but it can be a main dish, too. Goes well with just about anything. Serves 6-8

NANCY SULLIVAN

White-haired and sparkling-eyed, Nancy Sullivan of Stinson Beach is an avid hiker, canoeist, gardener, and lover of travel. "I was married to an adventurer," she said matter-of-factly, "It's the best way to learn, to travel, don't you think?"

She's big on education. "Only in the US do people say they've *finished school*," said Sullivan. She has been studying horticulture and is now a docent at the Strybing Arboretum. On one trip she studied tropical vegetation with a friend in Australia, New Zealand, Tasmania and Fiji. "I wanted to go to the home of the *Boronea Metastygma*.," she explained.

"It's a plant native to Southern Australia. It's an ugly plant, with needle-shaped leaves and small brown bells, but the fragrance is heavenly, like freesias or Chanel No. 5."

Such curiosity has taken her far and wide. "I went to Europe for three months to meet all the people in my family in England. Then I went to Budapest and Hungary where I met a woman who was just my age, doing all the things I like to do. We had no common language, but we understood each other perfectly. We still send each other greetings."

Language is no barrier to Sullivan. She shrugged and said, "Life everywhere is basically the same. Maybe it's easier for an older woman, like me. I love the challenge of travel and I love meeting new people. I've been traveling all my life. My youngest daughter was born in Japan."

She wasn't always so bold, she said, allowing that she was downright shy as a student at Tamalpais High. She entered UC Berkeley with the desire to be a landscape architect, like her uncle who had made a name for himself in the field. "But he said it was no field for a woman" explained Sullivan. "So I went into pre-med." With a strong background in science, she turned to psychology, worked as a social worker in Berkeley, and later as a school teacher.

Sullivan heads up what she calls a "gentleman's farm," in the valley, where a staff of people are growing "things you don't find in the markets — pink pearl apples, special varieties of roses and wildflowers, nut trees, a vegetable garden with better tomatoes, better basils. My favorite are the scarlet runner beans, sauteed in olive oil," she enthused.

As I rose to leave, she invited me to swim with her in the Bolinas Lagoon — a healthy one-half mile. "I'm driven to swim everyday," she said. "I take my fins down. The lagoon is 10 degrees warmer than the ocean and it's calm."

Here is one of her most requested recipes, first tasted at one of Sullivan's many memorable potluck dinners in Stinson Beach.

Carrot Cashew Curry

Ingredients:

4 Tbsp. butter
3-4 cloves crushed garlic
1 tsp. freshly minced ginger
1 tsp. mustard seeds
1 tsp. ground cumin
1 tsp. ground coriander
1 tsp. dill weed
1 tsp. turmeric
2 cups sliced red onion
2 small potatoes, sliced
4 large carrots, thinly sliced
2 cups orange juice
1 tsp. salt/cayenne pepper
2 red bell peppers, sliced
1-1/2 cups toasted cashews
1/2 cup raisins, optional
1 cup yogurt

Method:

Sauté garlic, ginger, mustard seeds in butter in a deep skillet, until the seeds pop. Add the rest of the spices, onions, potatoes and carrots and sauté for 5-8 minutes. Add orange juice. Cover, simmer 10-15 minutes. Add cayenne, peppers, and cashews. Simmer for 3-4 minutes. Stir in the yogurt just before serving. Serve over rice.

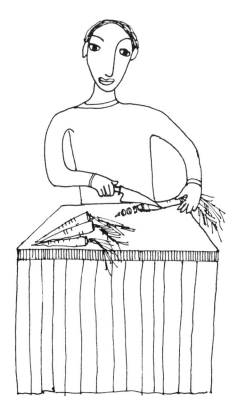

ARMIN ROSENCRANZ

Author, philanthropist and professor of environmental law, Armin Rosencranz of Inverness has championed environmental protection since the early 70s. He is an internationally recognized authority on global pollution issues such as acid rain, the greenhouse effect, and ozone depletion. His book, *Acid Rain in Europe and North America,* came out shortly after the scientific community first acknowledged the phenomenon of acid rain, a condition causing the death of forests as well as aquatic ecosystems. His research pointed to the presence of "acid fog" in West Marin as well.

Among his present projects is the Pioneer Fund, a private foundation for experienced, but unrecognized, documentary filmmakers of social or political relevance.

Under a Ford Foundation grant, he is writing a "case book on how to use the legal system to protect the environment."

And for two years Rosencranz has served as president of the Pacific Energy and Resources Center, a think tank of environmental experts located in the Marin Headlands.

"My main concern is the depletion of the ozone layer by chloro-fluorocarbons (cfcs), which also contribute to global warming," he said. "Cfcs are extremely stable. Once they do damage to the lower atmosphere, trapping heat, they migrate to the upper stratosphere and combine chemically with ozone molecules. If we stopped production of cfcs today, we'd still have to deal with already produced cfcs for the next 30 to 50 years as they continue to destroy the ozone layer."

The four main contributors of cfcs to the atmosphere are auto and home air conditioners (25 percent of the problem), refrigerator and freezer units, computer solvents and cleaning agents, and blowing agents in the production of rigid foams, insulation, styrofoam and building materials. "Those blue freezing containers are a real contributor. They break down and go directly into the environment," he said.

"The industrial nations are in agreement to stop the production of cfcs. Even the Soviet Union is committed to cfc phase out. But the problem is that we haven't involved the developing countries, which are rapidly modernizing. From thier point of view, we should subsidize the use of alternative substances. After all, they argue, nothing works as well in refrigeration and cooling as cfcs.."

"I was in the Soviet Union in an environmental forum," Rosencranz continued.. "The Soviets were delighted to make contact with the scientific community, but there is little awareness of global pollution as an issue. In Russian there is no word for environmental protection — it is nature protection or "ecologie," with more concern for species protection. What we did was to raise their consciousness so that they realize their stake is as great as ours."

Armin Rosencranz also cooks. Here is his recipe:

Armin's 15-Minute Vegetable Curry

Ingredients:

2 medium onions, diced
3 cloves chopped garlic
8-10 oz. frozen peas
6 cubed, steamed red potatoes
8 oz. chopped cauliflower or broccoli
8 oz. low-fat yogurt
2 T. garam masala
cayenne pepper
cinnamon
lemon juice

Method:

Sauté onions and garlic in oil in a large skillet. Add potatoes, peas, cauliflower and/or broccoli. In a mixing bowl, combine yogurt with garam masala (a sweet Indian curry spice).

Add dashes of cayenne pepper, cinnamon and lemon juice. Add yogurt mixture to skillet. Stir, simmer and serve.

Banana or Cucumber Raita

Ingredients:

3 bananas or 3 cucumbers
2 cups plain lowfat yogurt
cayenne pepper (to cucumber raita)

Method:

Slice three bananas and mash them in a bowl. Add two cups of yogurt. This is all you need for a sweet banana raita.

For cucumber raita, peel and grate cucumbers, add to yogurt and sprinkle red cayenne pepper on top.

BOBBIE LIKOVER

Going to the dentist has a whole new feeling to it, since I went to Bobbi Likover, DDS. What's so different? For one thing, she is a woman dentist. For another, her husband Lewis is her assistant. And the office, though appointed with state of the art equipment, looks and feels more like a wood-paneled living room.

The Likovers have created their office, which is adjacent to their home in Bolinas, with care. "I wanted to simplify my own practice. I feel that I can give better care to my patients in a less stressful environment. And this way, I can work three to four days a week, with time available for emergencies and spillover appointments."

Bobbi feels she can give better care by cleaning her patient's teeth herself. "I get more of a feel for the person's mouth and what is going on if I do the cleaning," she said. "I also do a complete diagnostic check for gum disease at that time. I do oral surgery, root canals, X-rays — I do everything except for orthodontia."

Before coming to Bolinas, Bobbi worked in a wholistic dental practice in Sebastopol, working with chemically or environmentally sensitive people. Some people, she said, may be sensitive to mercury vapors. In Sweden, they've banned the silver amalgam material to pregnant woman and issued warnings to the general public.

Bobbi has been practicing for 12 years, in various kinds of practices. "I try to make information available to my clients, especially those concerned with the effect of metals (fillings) and mercury on the body. We offer alternative substances to the amalgams, a filling made of composite resin, and of course, gold."

Her husband Lewis, whose original training is in social work, is learning the dental business from his wife, setting up the appointments, and handling the business end as well as assisting with actual dental work. They have developed a smooth and professional rapport with each other in the office.

Both Lewis and Bobbi came from "old left wing" families. "We're both 'red-diaper babies,' said Lewis. "I mean, both of us were born in the McCarthy era with parents accused of being red."

"I come from a strong feminist background where there were no limits on what a woman could do," said Bobbi, who grew up in Baltimore, and went to the University of Maryland Dental School. "It hasn't been easy to be a woman in the profession. It is one profession which is extremely patriarchal."

Here are three potato recipes the Likovers recommend.

Three Potato Recipes

Lewis Likover's Leftovers

Ingredients:

leftover potatoes, steamed or baked, cubed
onions, chopped
garlic, chopped
red, yellow and green peppers, diced
chili powder
salt and pepper, to taste
Parmesan cheese, grated

Method:

Sauté onions and garlic in butter. Add yellow, green and red peppers. Add potatoes, season with chili powder, salt, pepper. Sprinkle with Parmesan cheese and cover on low heat for 10 minutes.

Oven-Baked Dill Potatoes

Ingredients:

6-10 small, new potatoes
3-4 Tbsp. olive oil
Dried or fresh dill
salt and pepper to taste

Method:

Preheat oven to 375. Cut potatoes in chunks. Put in a bowl. Toss with olive oil, dill and salt and pepper. Put in a casserole dish. Put in the oven, tossing after 20 minutes. Toss again after 15 minutes, and continue baking untiil potatoes are crisp and oven fried. Serves four.

Potato Latkes

Ingredients:

2-3 large russet potatoes
1/2 onion
1-2 eggs
2-3 Tbsp. flour
olive oil
salt & pepper to taste
garnish with apple sauce and/or sour cream

Method:

Coarsely grate potatoes. Put in a bowl. Wring out extra water by placing them in a paper towel wrap. Grate onion.
Mix potatoes with eggs and flour. Blend together until a thick consistency. Place spoonful on a hot oiled griddle. Smack it down with a spatula until it is thin. Fry over medium low heat for 7-8 minutes a side. Serve with sour cream and/or apple sauce.

SUSAN ENGLEBRY & JEFF CREQUE

Tucked away in a tiny valley about a half mile past the Commonweal Gate on the way to the Palo Marin Trailhead is Bolinas's Laughing Duck Farm, also known as Commonweal Garden. Jeff Creque and Susan Englebry are dedicated organic farmers who live on and care for the farm.

"We specialize in fruits," said Susan, "although Jeff keeps a small vegetable garden. I focus on my flower business." We sat on the veranda of their small farmhouse, where I noticed swallows nesting above our heads. "Did you know that each swallow will produce 60 pounds of manure per season? I just shovel it up and compost it. They also eat mosquitoes," she added with a smile.

"Flowers are my main effort. I do bouquets for weddings, celebrations and retreats at Commonweal." She inquired, "Do you remember being a small child in a big flower garden? How they towered over you, engulfing you in their scent and color? That's what I envision here ... narrow paths with towering flowers everywhere. And my dream is to be an old woman who looks after volunteers in the garden. The abundance over the years of so many varieties of seed will ensure the flowers sow themselves."

We wandered through the gardens to find Jeff near the "glass house" in which crops of basil and tomatoes thrived. "My objective here is not pro-

duction," he explained, adding to Susan's description of their philosophy, "but an elusive concept of fertility. It's based on Fukuoko's idea which he called, 'Do Nothing Farming;' meaning, actually that you do only what you need to do; that nature and the wild environment is your teacher, already perfectly balanced."

A nemesis to the new orchard were the three families of foxes that moved in to feast on the fruit. "We're what you'd call a biological sink here. Like most cultivated areas, we draw everything from around — foxes, raccoons, blue jays, and gophers who come for easy living off our efforts," said Jeff.

But since they got "Batty", a fox terrier, the foxes have disappeared. There are four gopher-loving cats in the garden now. But a new frustration is blue jays, who eat only the crowns of ripening apples. "The answer is to produce more, so proportionately the loss isn't as great," said Jeff.

Jeff's orchard includes 40 varieties of apples, 35 varieties of pears and plums, prunes, figs, lemons, walnuts, persimmons, filberts, almonds and pinenuts. He often sells his delicious honey at the Bolinas People's Store.

Susan gives us this recipe for pesto, adding that the secret to its goodness is in the tearing of the basil leaves and smashing of the tomatoes with your hands which unlocks the flavors.

Farm-Style Pesto

Ingredients:

handful pine nuts
3 full sprigs of fresh basil leaves
2 large tomatoes
1/2 to 1/3 cup olive oil
coarse salt to taste
your favorite pasta
Parmesan cheese

Method:

Bring a large pot of water to boil, and immerse pasta, cooking according to directions. In the meantime, crumble and break a handful of pine nuts into a bowl. Tear leaves from 2 full sprigs of basil into tiny bits. Cut 2 tomatoes into bits. Cover with 1/2 to 1/3 cup olive oil. Mix with hands. Sprinkle with coarse salt to taste. Serve by spooning over steaming hot pasta. Sprinkle Parmesan cheese on top.

CLAIRE HEART

Lucky Bolinas. Any lover of food would agree, the Bolinas People's Store is truly a cornucopia, a lavish display of nature's best. This little gem of a store just gets better and better. From its rustic beginnings as a vegetable cart on Wharf Road, to the tiny, tin-roofed space behind the Community Center, the store has evolved through continual upgrading and redesigning.

Claire Heart, one of the 18 workers in the collective, is proud of the store and loves working there. "We have the best food and the best music in town," she boasts. On "run" days, twice a week, she leaves at 1 a.m. in the store's truck, bound for San Francisco's produce terminal.

First stop is an all-women's collective for organic vegetables. "I actually taste every box of corn myself. I have high standards — I grew up in the midwest." Next stop is for commercial produce, ("What we can't get at the organic place"), then bread, tortillas, and lastly bagels, before heading home. At 6:30 a.m. other workers greet the truck to help unload and stock.

"When I started work-ing here, the store was of a 'co-op" mind,' she recalled. "In the 70s the idea was cheap, bulk food. Now we're starting to figure out how to make things more convenient. We sell more ready-made products, like Weber's salad mix, or hummous. You could make them yourself, but people are busy.

"Shoppers are not shy in letting workers know what changes they do and don't like. They say, 'Oh wow, those cherries were (or were *not*) delicious!' We try to put the growers' names on the produce, so that people have a closer connection to the source of their food. We know where most of the food in our store is grown. We've been to the farm, talked to the farmer. And we know what's coming in."

"It's hard to figure out what's safe to eat," she said. "We are all pretty involved in the politics of food." Radiation of dairy products imported from Europe [from Chernobyl] is one of their concerns. The collective decided not to buy Mexican produce, not only because of high pesticide levels, but also because of exploitation of farm workers. Food irradiation is another issue they are fighting hard against.

During our discussion in the busy plaza in front of the store, Claire had answered a dozen questions, held a shopper's baby and given her son a snack. "It's not Safeway," she said, happily. "After five, some say it's as close to a single's bar as you'll find in West Marin."

Claire gave us this delicious recipe for eggplant, which she says is so tasty kids ask for more.

Sarah Hart, a worker at the People's store, contributed this recipe for Seitan, a kind of tofu-like patty, but made from wheat gluten.

Claire Heart's Eggplant Patties

Ingredients:

1 large eggplant
1 finely chopped onion
1/2 lb. grated Swiss cheese
2 crumbled slices of bread or wheat germ
oil for frying
flour for dredging

Method:

Cut a large eggplant in cubes. Steam or simmer until soft in saucepan. Drain. Mash and mix with chopped onion, grated Swiss cheese, and bread or wheat germ (to bind). Mash and shape into patties. Dip in flour, fry until crisp and brown on each side.

Lemon Seitan
from Sarah Allison Hart

Ingredients:

1-2 cloves garlic, minced
1/2 medium onion, finely diced
2-3 Tbsp. olive oil for frying
1/4-1/2 cup light vegetable oil
1 package Seitan (wheat gluten patties)
1/2-1 cup white wine
1-3 Tbsp. soy sauce or tamari
1-2 tsps. favorite mustard
1 tsp. dried basil
1 tsp. dill
1/2 tsp. tarragon
salt and pepper to taste
lemon, thinly sliced

Method:

Sauté garlic and onion in a saucepan with olive oil until slightly browned. Remove from pan and set aside.
Pour enough light oil in pan to cover bottom. Heat to medium-high. Place seitan slices in saucepan and brown a bit. Add garlic and onions and wine, soy and mustard. Simmer on medium heat to reduce liquid. Add basil, dill and tarragon. Sprinkle with salt & pepper to taste. Place slices of lemon on seitan slices. Cover and simmer.
Serve with brown and wild rice, seasoned with vegetable broth and tamari. Optional: sprinkle with pine nuts or almonds and sliced mushrooms.

SHA SHA HIGBY

Sculptural costume designer and dancer Sha Sha Higby sanded a smooth white mask as softly, almost shyly, she explained the process of creating her elaborate, intricate costumes, such as the one adorning a child-sized dummy before me.

If you haven't yet seen her work, you are in for an inspirational visual delight. Her solo performances are mesmerizing, often languid movements (sometimes acrobatic if the costume allows) accompanied by fragrance, bells, a minimal musical score, or the audience itself, using instruments made by Higby.

Sha Sha has shown and performed her work throughout Europe and this country. She recently toured Belgium, Holland, England and Switzerland with 10 performances. She's a Fulbright scholar, and spent five years in Java studying mask-making and dance. She spent one full year in Japan studying Noh mask making. In the Bay Area, she can be seen at places like the Marin Headlands, Mt. Tam, galleries such as the Hatley Martin, Langdon Gallery and at schools and festivals.

The inspiration for the dance, the costumes, are each the result of more than a year's meticulous work. The headpieces are constructed of up to three masks, or sometimes a splitface, not easily identified under fronds and winged departures — hundreds of tiny, carefully hand-sewn and dyed individual shapes of silk and chiffon. She uses only natural fabrics and subtle-colored dyes; the result is a patina with an ancient feel to it. Sewn in are bits of porcelain, tiny fans, accordion-like strings of hand-made pieces, tiny buttons, even tiny lights which, during a performance, she switches on.

The accessories to each piece are yet another matter, as in *Cows Under a Pepper Tree* where she is surrounded by tiny hand-painted houses, lit from inside and visited by small toy creatures that emerge on elastic string from beneath her layers.

In a recently made MTV videotape of *A Bee on The Beach*, she emerges a prehistoric butterfly (from behind a rock in the fog), undulating, expanding and contracting, and finally shedding the costume, like a lobster ridding his shell, and rolling away, a vulnerable, painted naked human.

"What I would like to achieve in a performance," said Higby, "is that if people come in a low state, that they would leave feeling lighter, and in a more hopeful space."

Sha Sha loves to make sushi and also gives us her garbanzo bean recipe:

Sha Sha's Spinach Sushi

Ingredients:

1 lb. steamed, squeezed, chopped spinach
gomasio (tamari and sesame seeds)
steamed rice (white, sticky rice works best)
1/4 cup rice vinegar
1 Tbsp. honey
1 package of nori (Japanese dried seaweed)
wasabi (Japanese horseradish paste)

Method:

Gomasio:
To make your own gomasio, first toast 1 cup of sesame seeds in a toaster oven or in a dry frying pan tossing often. In a nut and seed grinder or blender, grind seeds. Add drops of tamari, approximately a teaspoonful.
Sushi:
Mix the spinach with gomasio. Spread some hot rice on a sheet of nori (dried seaweed). Spread spinach on rice. Mix 1/4 cup rice vinegar with 1 tablespoon honey. Sprinkle spinach with vinegar/honey mixture. Roll up and eat with wasabi paste and tamari.

Sha Sha's Baked Garbanzos

Ingredients:

1 quart cooked garbanzos (or canned)
salt and pepper
3 large tomatoes, chopped
1 large onion, chopped
1 clove garlic, minced
1 tsp. rosemary
1/2 cup olive oil

Method:

If you cook the garbanzos yourself, use a pressure cooker and cook until soft. Put garbanzos in a baking dish. Combine the chopped tomatoes, onion, garlic, rosemary and olive oil. Spread on top of garbanzos. Bake at 375 degrees for 45-60 minutes.

DAN ROGOFF

Dan Rogoff of Bolinas watched so much TV when he was a kid that his sister dubbed him "TV Danny." But all those years glued to the tube may yet pay off. Rogoff, inspired by an article about public access TV in the Sunday *Chronicle*, looked over at his wife one day and said, "Let's make television."

Today he is the proud creator, writer and director of the "Uncle Butch Show," with 13 episodes on line.

"It's a rock 'n roll Mr. Rogers or maybe more like an Ed Sullivan of the 90s," Rogoff explained. "It's a show for kids that doesn't amp them up, but actually winds them down for bedtime. Our goal was to make the transition to bedtime easier."

The main character, Uncle Butch, is a "crusty unlikely star of a kid's show" who spends his days with wizards, wee folk, troubadours and fantasy characters such as King Banderstone and Lavender Leopard Lamberdeen. Butch is, in reality, a storyteller, writer and Marin Theatre Company actor who volunteered for the part.

Butch's best friend is the Music Man, Ron, a coffee shop — philosopher-storyteller who is inclined to break into song, played by Ron Elliott, once the lead singer and songwriter of the Beau Brummels (Laugh, Laugh). Elliott wrote the original scores for the show.

"These guys get together and sit and talk about simple things — like friendship and fear. They've known each other for a long time. They reminisce and sing together," explained Rogoff.

Interspersed between Butch and Ron's dialogue are video spots of jugglers, acrobats, electronic body music, and various interludes. One spot is blacksmith Dan Breaux of Nicasio shoeing a horse. Another is teenage Merlin Gaspers, talking about whether it's right to fight or walk away. He's playing basketball with a friend, who says, "Hey, you backed off it, man." But Merlin says, "You've got to put out the fire before it spreads." Another is the creation of a painting. At the the close of the show Butch tells an original bedtime story and sings a lullaby accompanied by a saxophone solo.

"It's a show for baby-boom families — geared for 5- to 10-year-olds, but teenagers and adults will like it for the music and the conversational content," said Rogoff.

Rogoff's work has always had to do with communication and kids. He was a Saul Alinsky-based community organizer, then counselor and teacher of teenage boys. He worked as an editor at Shelter Publications for two years and began writing — for *The Pacific Sun*, then publishing six novels for teens with low-level reading skills. At Viacom in Marin, he learned to use video equipment, and found an eager crew from among his artist and theater friends. Rogoff's wife, Marianne, is co-producer; but their 10-month-old son, Duncan, is the real inspiration for the Uncle Butch Show.

In the kitchen, Dan is known for his delicate touch. He offers us this recipe:

Rhoda's Broccoli Pie

Ingredients:

10 oz. broccoli, chopped
10 oz. grated sharp cheddar cheese
3 eggs, beaten
2 Tbsp. onions, chopped
2 Tbsp. butter
2 Tbsp. flour
wheat germ
almond slices

Method:

Toss broccoli and cheese in a bowl. Beat eggs with a whisk, then add to broccoli and cheese. Sauté onions in butter, sprinkling in flour. Add to cheese and eggs. Reach in with hands, mix thoroughly. Put in 8-inch greased pie pan. Sprinkle with wheat germ. Salt and pepper to taste. Top with almond slices. Bake at 325 degrees for 20 minutes covered, and 20 minutes uncovered, so as not to burn the almonds. Serve with a salad of red-leaf lettuce, pears and raisins, with a baguette, a bottle of white wine, and Al Green on the stereo.

SANDY & DENNIS DIERKS

Organic farmers of West Marin have long been aware of the problems with the use of chemicals in agriculture. Sandy and Dennis Dierks, organic vegetable farmers in Paradise Valley, have farmed the valley for nearly 20 years. They helped found the North Coast Chapter of California Certified Organic Farmers (CCOF) 15 years ago. The Marin chapter now includes six farms; five are in Bolinas.

"Up until a few years ago, it was commercially unheard of to farm organically. Organic gardening, but not farming," said Dennis. "There was no demand for it. You grew what you needed and gave the rest to neighbors."

Now it's a different story, and the demand for organic produce has come from the consumer: "Restaurants have had a lot to do with increased awareness of quality of produce," he said. "Safeway and Lucky supermarkets are also buying CCOF produce."

Recognizing the obvious potential for fraudulent labeling, the CCOF drafted a law eight years ago making the misrepresentation of organic produce a misdemeanor. Only now is the state assisting in its enforcement. They've had to carefully defined the term "organic."

The CCOF has been a grassroots organization — members monitor each other to make sure that everyone who claims to be organic is. The philosophy of CCOF is concerned not only with crop growth and yield but also with soil management, fertility and care, as the land will be passed on for generations.

"It's great to see such concern for organic produce, but on the other hand we're sorry to see the motivation be profit-making only," said Sandy Dierks.

"Agribusiness is beginning to get curious; some farmers are switching over to organic methods because the chemical thing isn't working," said Dennis. "They need more sprays each year because the bugs become resistant; the chemicals get too expensive."

Does organic food taste better? Safeway conducted a taste testing to find out. "They sampled produce that was unsprayed, Nutri-clean, commercial and CCOF certified. They found that in every case, the CCOF produce was not only better tasting, but visually more pleasing and generally higher quality," said Sandy. "You can buy Mexican produce that is perfect looking, but it's been repeatedly saturated and sprayed with chemicals."

Consumers can help stimulate the enforcement of standards for organic produce. Sandy urged, "Talk to your produce buyer. Ask where and how the produce was grown. Make the farmer accountable. I was surprised to get answers like, 'I don't know. It came through the distributor,' or, 'They said it was natural.' "

Here's a recipe from the Dierks' organic farm:

Italian Tomato Fennel

Ingredients:

3 fennel bulbs, sliced
3 tomatoes, skinned, sliced
breadcrumbs
1 clove garlic, sliced
1/4 cube butter
1 Tbsp. lemon
olive oil

Method:

Cut the fennel bulb in thin slices. Singe the tomatoes over flame and skin (or quickly steam and skin). Sauté fennel and garlic in olive oil until translucent. Add tomatoes, simmer for 10 minutes. Put in a casserole dish, sprinkle with breadcrumbs, squeeze on lemon, cut up butter on top. Bake in oven at 350 degrees for 20 minutes, or until lightly browned.

Michael Sykes

His office narrowly escaped the fire which charred the Western Saloon downstairs. Had the arsonist's blaze burned a few minutes longer, it would have put an end to his small publishing business in Point Reyes Station. Floating Island publisher Michael Sykes and I marveled at how little damage actually occurred to his offices. Books left on top of stacks were discolored from smoke, but the expensive collectors' edition books in Sykes' cabinets were spared.

Sykes' publishing company, Floating Island, is so named "because geographically, Point Reyes peninsula is actually an island, floating slowly toward the Aleutian trench," Sykes explained. The firm has been in business for 13 years, and has published some 30 books. The original idea was to publish a quarterly collection of work by local poets and writers, called "Floating Island."

"But it was too expen-sive, too expansive and just too much work to do quar-terly," said Sykes with a smile. "We just published Volume No. IV, 13 years later." It's a beautifully designed, softbound book featuring prose and poetry by 23 writers such as Robert Bly, Gary Snyder and Joanne Kyger, and interspersed with photographs.

The criteria for publication by Floating Island, are both unique and basic. "I need to have a rapport with the writer," explained Sykes, "whose work I like; but which also gives me an opportunity to use type and design and art work in a complimentary way. The author needs to be actively committed to the work of distribution and promotion — willing to give readings, work out mailing lists, and that sort of thing."

Sykes grew up in a house full of books on Cape Cod. His father, a Princeton scholar in French literature, urged him to read the classics. "I resisted them hard," recalled Sykes, "but I loved science fiction — the old 1950s Sci Fi — and that's when I began to love to read."

He learned that San Francisco State had a first-rate writing school, so headed west for college. At 18, Sykes found San Francisco exotic, his days spent in North Beach, at the City Lights Bookstore, absorbing writers such Kerouac and Ferlinghetti, along with jazz and poetry.

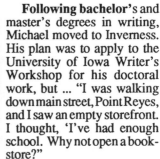

Following bachelor's and master's degrees in writing, Michael moved to Inverness. His plan was to apply to the University of Iowa Writer's Workshop for his doctoral work, but ... "I was walking down main street, Point Reyes, and I saw an empty storefront. I thought, 'I've had enough school. Why not open a bookstore?"

That storefront became the Punta de Los Reyes Bookstore, a place frequented by local writers and artists, like Bill Berkson, Bobbie Louise Hawkins, Aaron Saroyan and Robert Bly.

"The whole time I wanted to publish, and had that in mind. But the bookselling business didn't allow for the time. So I sold it in 1974."

Sykes offers us his recipe for Near Eastern vegetarian stuffed grape leaves. The tradition is to use ground lamb, but these satisfy any craving for protein. Ideally they should be served chilled.

Michael Sykes' Stuffed Grape Leaves

Ingredients:

2 jars grapeleaves
3 chopped onions
4 cups uncooked brown rice
head garlic, minced
1/2 lb. cashew pieces
salt, pepper
1/2 lb. golden raisins
2 Tbsp. dried oregano
2 Tbsp. cumin
2 Tbsp. curry powder

Method:

Sautée onions and garlic in olive oil in a big pot. Add brown rice, saute until coated with oil. Add water, salt, pepper, and oregano. Stir, bring to a boil, cover and turn to low for 45 minutes. When rice is cooked, put it in a bowl, mix in raisins, cashews, cumin and curry. Rinse grapeleaves. Lay one flat. Roll a heaping tbsp. of rice filling, folding into tubular packet. Place in a large Chinese bamboo steamer. Cover and steam over skillet of boiling water for 30 minutes. Chill and serve with sour cream, dill and slices of lemon. Makes 120 morsels.

MARGARET GRAHAM & WALTER EARLE

What drought-resistant plants can we plant in West Marin that would have a remote chance of survival, given the deer and gopher population?

This is precisely the sort of tough question Margaret Graham and Walter Earle of the Mostly Natives Nursery in Tomales are ready for. And their expert advice is free.

The nursery, located on a quarter acre right on Highway 1, is dedicated to the propagation and sale of plants which are suited to the cool coastal climate of West Marin. Everything sold is grown on the premises — plants which are drought resistant, deer resistant and hardy. There are flowering perennials, shrubs, ground covers, native grasses and trees, along with vegetable-garden starts and herbs. And true to the name, 60 percent of stock is native to the area.

Starting their own nursery was a solution to a propagation problem itself. "When we bought plants from nurseries inland, especially those from the Central Valley, they went through tremendous shock on the coast," explained Graham. "So we decided to grow them here."

The growers are active in the Native Plant Society and the California Horticultural Society. Always looking for new plants, they occasionally buy cuttings from the Saratoga Horticultural Foundation in South San Jose, a plant research and testing station. "Our goal is to get new native plants into the nurseries. But we also keep our own stock as a propagating source," he added.

"Native grasses are becoming very popular," Graham remarked. "We started them as a lark and sold out twice. We carry six varieties including one lawn substitute."

Few nurseries carry many trees, but they are Graham's favorites, especially the pretty blue-green Giant Sequoias, which grow well on the coast, the wind keeping the size down. They also have coastal redwoods, dwarf pines, bishops and several varieties of ornamental eucalyptus.

She mentioned other varieties too, like the ground cover Mahonia Repens or Creeping Oregon Grape, which takes no watering and deer hate. It has pretty yellow flowers and purple berries. Another was the showy, colorful Penstemons, English Lavender, which can grow in a hedgerow three-feet high, Mediterranean sun roses, Ceanothus (wild lilac in 10 varieties) and Manzanitas (6 to 8 varieties).

In the wintertime, when the growing season slows, Graham and Earle can be found out on Tomales Bay on a herring boat. They work for the Fish and Game Department, measuring the year's spawn by sampling random eel grass beds for eggs. "We actually met on the herring dock back in '81," Earle injected.

Both partners work outdoors all day. Two hungry youngsters — a four- and 15-year-old await with appetites to quell, so this is one solution:

Cream Cheese & Artichoke Heart Pizza

Ingredients:

1 Boboni pizza crust (or one you might make)
olive oil
1 package cream cheese
1 jar artichoke hearts
black olives
mushrooms
2 cloves fresh garlic, minced

Method:

Start with the pizza crust. Smear on olive oil. Spread on the soft cream cheese. Chop up marinated artichoke hearts, black olives, mushrooms and fresh garlic. Spread on crust. Bake at 375 degrees for 12-15 minutes.

AMLETO ROSSI

I was to dine with Amleto Rossi, renowned pizza chef of Bolinas and full-blooded Italian ("When you are born in Rome, you know, your family goes back as far as Caesar.") He was in his kitchen, patting dough gently onto a baking sheet when I arrived. We are going to have Focaccia... *[fo cot' cha]*, he said, "... the original pizza. They start putting one day the cheese, meat, sauce on the dough. But originally in Italy, they make like this."

I watched as he deftly moved about, describing the dish he was preparing. He was accompanied by strains of Italian opera ("Come back, my heart is waiting for you") and the *thunk* of solidly hit tennis balls on the courts across the street.

"It is important to use the very best olive oil," he said, drizzling this over the dough, from a quart bottle of cold pressed, extra-virgin olive oil. (Can anyone tell the difference between virgin and extra virgin?) "It is the key to cooking."

Freshly homemade pesto sauce was the next ingredient. Amleto reached into the refrigerator for a jar of it and wafted the fragrant basil-mixture past my nose, grinning as I sighed after it. Then he began spreading small spoonfuls onto the dough. Then he took out a large wooden mortar and pestle, poured in some rock salt, and began grinding.

"Do you know radicchio?" He offered me a tiny red leaf from an enormous bowl of baby lettuces, which he proceeded to drizzle with olive oil, tossing, drizzling, and tossing some more. A little ground pepper, coarse salt, and red wine vinegar. The pizza had also been dusted with coarse salt and was, from the aroma filling the air, about ready.

"Italians are born with art in life," he said. "I see cooking as art .... You don't have to go to school. You just use the best ingredients, and common sense. This dish is something you have got to see and taste. Also, I've got to have lunch."

We moved out to the second-story deck to the picnic table, where he uncorked a bottle of chardonnay to accompany the crispy pesto pizza slices and salad. Oh well, I thought, all in a day's work. After all... when in Rome ....

Amleto offers this recipe for focaccia. It is a very basic pizza recipe and there are as many variations on this recipe as there are for pizza toppings; sundried tomatoes, onion, mushrooms, anchovies or pesto. Ramarino is a version using rosemary and coarse salt for topping.

We have included his pesto recipe as well, because pesto is such a versatile ingredient in either pizza, focaccia or on pasta.

Homemade Pesto

Ingredients:

4 cups fresh basil
3 cloves garlic
salt
1-1/4 cups parmesan cheese
1/4 cup pine nuts
1 cup olive oil

Method:

Mix in a mortar and pestle: fresh basil, garlic cloves, salt, Parmesan cheese, pine nuts, olive oil. Grind into a paste. Spoon on top of hot pasta or pizza dough.

Focaccia

Ingredients:

1 pkg. active dry yeast
1/4 cup lukewarm water
1-1/2 tsp. sugar
2-1/2 tsp. salt
1/2 cup olive oil
1-3/4 cup hot water
6 cups all-purpose flour

Method:

Sprinkle dry yeast into warm water (use very warm water, 105-115 degrees) Let stand for a few minutes, then stir until dissolved. Put sugar, salt, oil in a bowl. Add hot water and stir. Cool to lukewarm. Stir in the yeast mixture. Add half of the flour and beat until smooth with a wooden spoon. Gradually stir in remaining flour. Divide dough into four portions. Let stand for one hour. Then roll each on a floured board to about 13 inches in diameter. Shape on a lightly greased 12-inch heavy gauge cookie sheet or pizza pan. Then spread the pesto mixture on the dough. Cook in a 425 degree oven for 15 to 20 minutes.

Ramarino

Ingredients:

Rosemary (Italian, fresh or dried)
Coarse kosher salt (crushed in mortar & pestle)
Olive oil

Method:

Prepare dough as in recipe above. Roll out to rounds and shape on a pan. With fork, poke holes in the dough, for oil to penetrate. Sprinkle dough with olive oil. Top with kosher salt. Sprinkle with rosemary. Bake in 425 degree oven for 15 to 20 minutes.

PINE GULCH CLASSROOM

A hand-colored, signed edition of the *Pine Gulch Dinnertime Cookbook* came into my hands this week. The cookbook contains "50 kid-approved recipes for the whole family" and is just one of the projects of the Pine Gulch Classroom kids in the Bolinas-Stinson Beach School District. The book will help fund a class and family trip to Yosemite.

The idea behind this cookbook, parent and project coordinator Lea Earnheart states, was "to put together a collection of dinner recipes that *everyone* in the family could enjoy together." Feeding kids is not always an easy task, she said, and satisfying adults with a dinner menu at the same time as the kids is even tougher.

So each of the 23 kids in the classroom (pictured here) came up with three recipes which both adults and kids in their homes liked to eat for dinner. It is beautifully hand-printed by Lea Earnheart, with original graphics by the kids.

The book features recipes with delicious sounding names like Purple Soup, Soba noodles with Yummy Sauce, Fila Flowers (these kids absolutely love anything made with filo pastry dough), Spanikopita, Pizzatillas, Gangster Potatoes, Blintzes and Wontons.

Fourth grader Briana Buchanan has this year joined Pine Gulch's individuated, multi-level classroom (housed on the Bolinas campus) after spending grades one through three in the school district's regular academic program. When asked why she likes the Pine Gulch program, Briana answered, "When I wake up in the morning to go

to school I know that every day will be different. We go on field trips every week and Fridays are free choice days." She explained, "You have to choose between reading, math, or language and spelling, but you can do which one you want first."

Does she think she gets more or less work done than in the other classrooms? "The same," she said. How does it feel to take class with all age levels? "Actually it doesn't feel that different, because usually you're working with your own age group anyway."

But Briana did say that she wishes her friends from the other classrooms could come in for a week to see what it's like at Pine Gulch.

Pine Gulch's emphasis on "first-hand experience" includes field trips to places such as the Recycling Center in San Rafael during a class project on the environment. Studying about the Miwok Indians included a full-costume reenactment on Agate Beach of the landing of Sir Francis Drake. Drake was played by adult actor Howard Dillon.

The Pine Gulch program, which was begun in 1978, provides the students with lots of input from the community. Teachers Kathie Sweeney and Cathy Nicholini team-teach the program. But it is parent involvement that has enabled the program to thrive — allowing for individualized learning. In many cases, students study at levels above their grade level.

Here are two recipes from the *Pine Gulch Dinnertime Cookbook*:

Pine Gulch Wontons

Ingredients:

1 package wonton wrappers (you can get these at Safeway)
1/4 lb. (approximately) ground pork or chicken
1 8-oz. can bamboo shoots
1 8-oz can water chestnuts
2 cloves garlic
2 green onion stems
1 tsp. soy sauce
1 tsp. sesame oil
dash of black pepper

Method:

Mince finely the pork or chicken, bamboo shoots, water chestnuts, green onion and garlic. Mix everything together, adding remaining ingredients.

Place 1 tsp. of mixture near left corner of wrapper., and roll up tightly, leaving right corner unrolled like this.

Gently fold the two ends over and stick them together with a dab of water. When you've got them all made, deep fry in peanut oil until golden brown. Drain on paper towels.

Soba Noodles and Yummy Sauce

Ingredients:

1 package Japanese Soba noodles
1/4-1/3 cup tamari
3 Tbsp. tahini
1-2 Tbsp. honey

Method:

Prepare soba noodles according to directions on package. Mix tahini, honey and tamari together with a fork. Add a little water if you need to. Spoon over noodles.

NINA PHILLIPS

With 15 years experience as a professional cook and caterer, Nina Phillips of Bolinas specializes in natural, vegetarian food, organically grown, seasonal and local whenever possible. Her private catering business, called *Naturally Nina's,* serves mouth-watering dishes, often vegetarian but always light and artistically arranged, and usually of an ethnic persuasion, such as Chinese, Middle Eastern, or East Indian.

An alumni luncheon Nina recently catered featured a simple Chinese menu — rice-stick baskets filled with Chinese chicken salad, mixed green salad with oriental dressing, Szechuan soba noodle salad with peanut chili sauce, toasted sesame seeds and cashews. "I added color with flowers and herbs I picked from the garden, things like borage, calendula, gladiolas, nasturtiums and scallion flowers all mounded up made it much prettier," she said.

"What I love about living in the country is finding wild herbs and berries. Wild rosemary and bay is prolific here. Whenever I can I'm out picking herbs or berries or fresh fruit to make jams or vinegars. I guess I'm what you'd call food obsessed. I also consult with people who want help making up menus or need recipes. They'll call me and say 'I've looked everywhere but I can't find that recipe for —' So I'll research the recipe."

Phillips's love for food began in her childhood, where food was central to every occasion. Raised in a kosher home in New York she recalls, "I never saw a frozen or fast-food product. Everyone in the family cooked. My dad used to make his own yogurt and borscht. My brothers cooked, too. I baked cookies, pies, cakes — always from scratch. I'm not sure how healthy it all was, but it sure tasted good. Even if it was only me visiting, my aunt would bring out a table full of food and insist I eat it all. Eating has always been a way of nurturing and giving love in my family."

Nina began large-scale cooking at an inn near her home in New Hampshire, serving and cooking for weddings, banquets, and buffets, in traditional New England style. Later she worked at a steak house chain where she suggested introducing a line of vegetarian quiches. It caught on fast and soon she was making over 100 quiches a day.

"I came to Bolinas for a two-week vacation and I've been here twelve years," she said with a smile. "The two places I've been the happiest are New Hampshire and Bolinas.... I'm a country girl at heart."

Here are two recipes from Naturally Nina's recipe collection:

Ratatouille Tart

Ingredients:

1 9" pie unbaked pastry shell
1/4 cup and 2 Tbsp. olive oil
1 onion, chopped
1 medium eggplant, peeled and diced
2 large cloves garlic, minced
1- 28 oz. can whole tomatoes, drained &
   chopped
1- 15 oz. can tomato sauce
2 Tbsp. fresh chopped basil or 2 tsp. dried
1/4 cup chopped parsley
1/2 tsp. sweetener (honey or sugar)
2 cups (about 1/2 lb.) Jarlsburg cheese
2 whole eggs
1 egg yolk
1/2 cup cream
1/4 cup Parmesan, grated

Method:

Bake pastry shell for 15 minutes or until bottom becomes golden. Cool on a rack until ready to use.In a saucepan, heat 2 Tbsp. olive oil and sauté onion until soft. Add 2 Tbsp. more oil and sauté eggplant over medium high heat, stirring often until soft. Add extra oil as needed. Stir in tomatoes, tomato sauce, basil, parsley, garlic and sweetener.

Cook uncovered, stir occasionally until the sauce is thickened and liquid absorbed.

Preheat oven to 375 degrees. Place oven rack in bottom third of oven. Sprinkle half the Jarlsburg cheese in thepastry shell, then layer withsauce mixture. Whisk together eggs, egg yolk, and cream. Pour over the sauce mixture, leave room. Sprinkle with remaining Jarlsburg cheese and the Parmesan cheese.

Bake for about 25 minutes or until puffy and golden. Cool on a rack at least 10 minutes before serving. Serves 6-8.

Naturally Nina's Hummus

Ingredients:

4 cups cooked chick peas, drained
4 garlic cloves, minced
1/2 cup roasted tahini
1 tsp. salt or tamari to taste
1/3 cup warm chick pea stock
2 tsp. ground cumin
1/3 cup quality olive oil
cayenne
paprika
black pepper
juice of 2-4 lemons
Italian parsley, chopped

Method:

Gently sauté two or more garlic cloves in two tablespoons of olive oil for two minutes. Set aside. Mash chick peas, add tahini, mix well. Slowly add warm stock and 1/2 lemon juice. Mix in remaining olive oil. Add sautéed garlic, raw garlic, salt. Stir well. Add spices, parsley, lemon juice. Refrigerate. Serve with whole-wheat pita chips and carrot rounds.

MEAT & POULTRY

GEORGE SHUTZ

Composer/producer George Shutz was planning a Big-Apple style celebration at the Bolinas Community Center for Saturday night. The occasion? Fifty years on the planet is as good a time as any to make a career switch.

After producing 800 concerts for the likes of Jean Pierre Rampal, Keith Jarrett, Ravi Shankar, The Chieftains, and Oregon at places like Carnegie Hall and the Metropolitan Opera House in New York City, Shutz was ready to leave the producing world and return to his own musical compositions.

Shutz's training on the piano began at age three. By seven his strong suit was sight reading, but an accident damaging his eyes prevented him from continuing.

"When I was a teenager, I found jazz. I'd play it instead of my classical practice in the afternoon until I heard my father's key in the door. Then I'd switch back to classical. I guess one time my father stood outside the door and heard me playing jazz. He came in and told me it sounded good. Then he bought me records.... Brubeck, Jerry Mulligan, Gillespie. So in my late teens I had two completely different sets of friends. I had my jazz friends and my classical ones. They didn't mix. It was difficult.

But I felt comfortable in both circles.

"Then I met Leonard Bernstein when he was putting together the 'What is Jazz' series. It was produced by CBS's classical division. I was only 17, but they thought I was the perfect go-between."

Shutz became a liaison between musicians, with an eclectic taste for classical, jazz, folk, electronic, and ethnic forms of music, discovering new musicians and forming new groups like the Rochester Jazz Society — even as he studied for a psychology degree at the University of Rochester. "That's why I was successful, I think," said Shutz, "because I crossed over the lines. Now there's a lot more of that sort of thing."

It might also be the reason he is hard pressed to describe to producers what kind of music he plays. "The different editors for the record companies want to know what bin it'll go in in the record store. There's words like 'fusion' which mean more electric jazz rock, or 'New Age,' which tends to mean mellow mood music. They're wonderful words but have been used so much they don't mean much."

Born in Vienna, George gives us his recipe for Wienerschnitzel, adding, "This is best with lemon, followed by some dessert, preferably with lots of whipped cream on it."

George Shutz's Wienerschnitzel

Ingredients:

4 veal cutlets
2 eggs, beaten
1/2 cup flour
1/2 cup breadcrumbs
oil for frying

Method:

The secret is to take the veal cutlets and pound them until they are paper thin. Beat the two eggs. Then dip the cutlets in egg, then flour, then breadcrumbs, and place in a pan of preheated oil and fry until golden brown. Serve with a wedge of lemon.

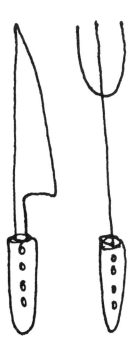

RUTH STOTTER

The art of telling tales is storyteller Ruth Stotter's profession, and her love for stories has led her on travels around the world in pursuit of learning still more. Stotter, a part-time Stinson Beach dweller, is the director and teacher of Dominican College's Storytelling Certification Program.

She's listened to stories in Peru, Japan, Alaska and Nepal. In 1980 she spent six weeks in Eskimo bush villages with the Artists-in-Schools program.

"My goal is to be invited home for dinner," she said, "even when my vocabulary is only a few hundred words. As a guest in Eskimo homes, I asked for ghost stories, and came home with 30 of them. But later I learned that they have 12 words for ghost, and I had only asked for one kind."

"The profession of storytelling is a service," she said. "Telling a story can help one understand the culture it came from. It is also an inter-disciplinary art; much is drawn from studies of linguistics, ethnic studies, anthropology, literature, history, art and theater. For instance, a Native American story begins: 'She left her husband and went back to her people ....' Without understanding this was a very dangerous thing to do in that culture, you can't understand the full impact of the statement."

"Many stories contain lessons and show how people in a culture cope with difficulty. For instance there's a story about a coyote who got stuck in a cedar tree. He tries four ways to get out. Then finally he takes himself apart. In other words, the solution to a problem isn't always to stay strong. It may be to fall apart. You might think it's a dumb little story, but if you understand the layers of meaning, you gain respect for the whole culture."

Stotter's effectiveness at making a story come alive goes back to her childhood. "When I was eight years old I was sent home from camp for telling scary stories," she said with a smile. "The girls were all wetting their beds." But at age 13 at the next camp, she was made camp storyteller. Since then she's told stories for radio shows, the Renaissance Fair, in bookstores and cafes, in schools and groups across the US, in England and Australia.

She adapts stories for all age levels, from pre-schoolers to senior citizens groups, and she sometimes tells her own "Cathryn Jane" stories.

To accompany her lamb recipe, Stotter recited: "Mary had a little lamb/ she covered it with soot./ So when she took it for a walk/ A sooty footy put."

Quick 'n Easy Tomato Lamb Curry

Ingredients:

Meatballs:
1-1/2 lb. ground lamb
1 minced onion
1/3 cup bread crumbs
1/2 tsp. pepper
1/4 cup milk

Sauce:
1 can whole tomatoes, with liquid
1/2 chopped onion
1 tsp curry powder
1/4 tsp. pepper
1/4 cup bread crumbs

Method:

Meatballs:
   Mix above ingredients, forming 3/4" meatballs. Brown in frying pan, pour off fat.

Sauce:
   In saucepan simmer tomatoes, onion, curry powder, pepper, and bread crumbs for 15 minutes: Add meatballs and serve over rice. Serves 3-4.

DAVE BRACHER

One foggy noontime, I was taken back to 16th century England — through latched doors to a fireside seat in the "snug room" of Muir Beach's Pelican Inn. The snug room is as its name suggests, with stuffed furniture arranged closely around a fireplace. Through the door came the muffled bustle of a busy roadside tavern, but this room made you expect to find an Elizabethan gentleman dallying with his lady. A cobblestone floor and dark, wood-beamed ceiling completed the feeling.

Charles Felix, the original owner and designer of the Pelican Inn, was a homesick Englishman who recreated this English Inn in complete detail, importing leaded English windows, brass knickknackery, furniture and decor. He went so far as to recreate a "Priesthole" which, during the days of Charles I, was built inside the dining room fireplace to hide Catholic priests in safety. Though the place feels ancient, the building was completed in only 1979. Felix has since sold the Inn and retired to England.

Smuggling and hiding of political dissidents during the 16th Century was common; in this case the King's supporters were in civil war against the "Parliamentarians" or "Roundheads" (who wore round metal helmets) protesting the "wrongful actions" of King Charles. The black band around the chimney of the Pelican Inn indicates it is a Royalist establishment, a safe hiding place for the "Cavaliers" or King's supporters.

"The story goes," manager Barry Stock said, "that Charles Felix had a female ghost that followed him around since he was a young man. This ghost was benevolent enough, but Felix reported waking up to her peering at him. Charles may have had something she was after, one cannot know, as sometimes ghosts are attracted to artifacts, and certainly there are many antiques here.

"Anyway, one night I was sitting and writing in that chair, using the lamp behind me to write by. There were only a few guests in the inn that night. The sensor lights, which respond to a clap or loud noise in the room by going on brighter, were on low. Well, room number 7 above me was unoccupied, but I heard footsteps across the floor above me so loud that the sensor lights came up. I didn't go up to find out what it was."

There have been at least two other such incidents, according to Stock. His wife has seen the ghost, in the form of a mist, and he says others have reported impossible sounds.

Through the latched door came chef Dave Bracher, the creator of true tavern vituals: Bangers and Mash, Beef Wellington, Standing Prime Rib, Rack of Lamb, Devonshire Chicken and Roast Duckling.

Vegetarian and seafood dishes, salads and homemade soups can also be found on the menu. You can get a pot of tea any time, with homemade trifle or bread pudding served warm with almonds and fresh whipped cream.

Bracher's is rumored to be the best Roast Duckling served anywhere. His Yorkshire Pudding is a classic recipe, except it is baked in individual servings.

Roast Duckling w/ Mint Cassis Sauce

Ingredients:

1 duck (cleaned)
1 cup duck stock (or brown sauce)
1/2 cup Creme Cassis (Black currant liqueur)
1 Tbsp. butter unmelted
1 Tbsp. fresh, chopped mint leaves

Method:

Pre-cook duck in a roasting pan for 2-1/2 hours at 350 degrees. Remove duck and cut in half. Remove bones (they should slide out easily). Put both halves back in oven on broil for 20 minutes (or until skin is crisp.)

In a sauce pan, put stock (duck drippings, fat drained off) and Cassis. Reduce, add butter and mint leaves, stir until thick. Pour over duck and serve.

Yorkshire Pudding

Ingredients:

1/2 cup of meat drippings from pan
8 eggs
2/3 cup flour
2/3 cup milk
1 tsp. each salt and pepper

Method:

Combine all of these ingredients and whip together until creamy. Bake in greased cupcake or muffin tins. Fill until almost full. Bake for 45 minutes at 375 degrees. It will puff up like a turnover. Can be baked in a large baking dish, but this way it yields individual servings.

LINDA & KEN MARSHALL

Rancho Nicasio is located on the north end of the Nicasio town square. It was created by early Mexican settlers in their own tradition, and remains today much as it was at the turn of the century — a traditional steak house and watering hole.

The history of land ownership in Nicasio is laced with unsavory exchanges; murder and perjury being fairly common ways to acquire property. The Miwok Indians were promised Nicasio land, and then swindled out of it in 1843 when Governor Manuel Micheltorena gave the land instead to Pablo de la Guerra and Juan Cooper.

The town square was formed by the building of St. Mary's Church, then the Nicasio Hotel, a stable, livery and the Druid's Hall, as more settlers came to the area, logging for redwood and oak, and ranching the land. Cow punching was an early activity in the town square, and in the early 1900s, baseball became the favored event. It still is.

Rancho Nicasio has been recently dubbed "Rancho Romance" because at least three couples have met, courted and found marital bliss while working at Rancho Nicasio for Linda and Ken Marshall, the new owners. That says something about the spirit and teamwork of the staff which has been hand-picked by these first-time restaurant owners.

The Marshalls brought the old steakhouse and bar to life, after the building sat idle for seven years. The spacious tavern has a western feel, with its swinging doors, long, polished wood bar, and mounted heads of elk and moose on the walls.

The restaurant once again is serving the traditional fare many old-timers remember it for — prime ribs, chicken, steak and potatoes in generous portions — as well as new dishes, including pastas, seafood dishes, rack of lamb, and original recipes by their new chef, Paul Irving.

There's music again now, too. But observing county noise regulations and town sentiment in favor of lower-key music, there is dancing only on Friday nights to 1940s swing and country music.

Ken grew up in the San Rafael area, and visited West Marin often in his youth. He is a retired fireman and building contractor, and is planning to build his own house near the restaurant in the not-too-distant future.

Linda is frequently called out of town to fly with American Airlines. She has been a flight attendant with American for 22 years. "I remember signing a waiver agreeing to retire at 32. I couldn't imagine ever being that old," she said shaking her head. "Since that time American has retracted those sexist policies.

"Sometimes, on a busy night at Rancho Nicasio, it feels just about like serving a fully loaded 747," she added. "There's just about the same number of people to take care of — somewhere between 200 and 300."

Chef Irving emerged from the kitchen and wrote down this "quite California" recipe, created with the kibbitzing of two other chefs, noting, "While this recipe sounds fancy, it is really very fast and simple, and relies on fresh ingredients."

Walnut-Pesto Chicken with Chevre

Ingredients:

1/4 cup chopped walnuts, lightly toasted
1/4 cup olive oil
3 cloves of garlic
2 cups chopped cilantro leaves
1/4 cup walnut oil
1/4 cup grated parmesan cheese
1/8 tsp. salt
 fresh ground black pepper to taste
 2 whole boneless, skinless chicken breasts (10-12 oz, pounded lightly so they will easily fold in half)

2 tomatoes
1/4 cup white wine
olive oil for frying
1-2 Tbsp. flour
1 oz. unsalted butter
 2-3 oz. chevre cheese

Method:

Blend together walnuts, olive oil, garlic, cilantro, walnut oil, Parmesan cheese and salt and pepper in a processor or blender until it becomes a smooth paste.

Spread the two flat sides of the chicken breast open and coat the inside of the breast with a thin layer of pesto, then fold in half, with pesto inside. Refrigerate to firm up, 5-10 min.

While the breast chills, blanch two tomatoes in salted boiling water, then peel the skins in an ice-water bath. Dice them (you may want to strain the seeds).

In a thick skillet over medium heat, add 1 T. olive oil per breast. Keeping the breast folded, dust the chicken with flour, shaking off the excess, then place into hot oil. When the first side has browned, turn them over and remove from heat.

Pour into the skillet: wine, diced tomatoes, about 1 tablespoon of pesto, stir, and place the skillet in a 350-degree oven for 5 min. (maximum).

Remove the breast onto a side plate.

Over medium-high heat, reduce the liquid by half volume and toss in the butter.

Put the chicken back in the skillet over the sauce, top with chevre to your liking (1-2 oz.) and place a lid over the pan to soften the cheese. You can place under a broiler for 20-30 seconds to melt cheese.

Now it is ready to serve, garnished with a sprig of cilantro.

PIERRE SALONE

"I never follow a recipe. I don't even have recipes. I go to the fridge and see what I have. It's up here." said Bolinas's French chef, Pierre Salone, pointing to his head. It was the morning after his semi-annual serving of Moroccan couscous for friends at his home.

We sat in his front room, partly because Pierre couldn't face the disaster in the kitchen (we said he *cooks* ....we did not say he was fast on cleanup) and partly because the room was warmed by a fire on this foggy morning.

Speaking very little English, Pierre moved to the US from Poussin, France, 10 years ago. Since then he has developed carpentry skills (to support his taste for the finer things), honed his culinary artistry (both commercially with Chez Madeleine and for his lucky friends) and most recently become "sportif," taking up mountain- bike riding (to get in shape).

"I don't want to give you the couscous (recipe) ... too complicated. If I give recipe for eight hource of cooking with two ounces of cumin, people will faint... and you won't have any room on your column."

"I want to give you something hot. I like Thai food a lot and I found this curry paste in the Bangkok market in the city. You can buy a can for under a dollar. We use the green curry paste. This is hot without killing you. Last week I used panang red curry paste and it's a dragon, oh, I tell you.

"Hot food is a trip. This doesn't mean you always burn your mouth. Some you feel on the tip of your tongue. Some other will heat the back of your tongue and your throat. And some heat you don't feel as it goes by but it comes from inside and you sweat and flush your face. Thai food is not just eating .... it's an intense experience. I think it makes you thin, sexy too.

"We do chicken. This makes chicken exciting and cheap. So, you need one chicken. Preferably one that is aged — the oldest, scrawniest chicken you can find so you can cook it a long time. If you were in France, you buy a rooster. Well, here you do the best you can ....

"Serve this curry chicken with steamed basmati rice because it tastes like peanuts a little bit. Believe me it's a good dish... Next I'm going to make duck with the panang red paste. That will be much hotter. It's more fun to make it different each time. I cook just for fun... and I love to talk about food."

Green Curry Chicken

Ingredients:

1 scrawny chicken, cut into pieces
peanut oil
butter
3 onions, thinly sliced
4 oz. can green curry paste
1/4 pint chicken stock
1 can coconut milk
2 bananas
fresh (of course, *always*) basil, one bunch
plum jam (I use my own pineapple jam)
salt and pepper

Method:

First, you start with peanut oil (to keep the heat) and butter (for taste). You sautée the onions, which are very thinly sliced, not chopped, for about 40 minutes. You start on high and go low. But don't burn them. You keep stirring until they are a cream. This is a secret. When the curry is done you have chicken and sauce, nothing else.

Then, ten minutes before onions are finished, you start sautéeing chicken in a stew pot... peanut oil again until it is brown. The chicken is kot. Kot? Kot! Kot! When you go to the butcher it is whole or kot! Now add the green curry paste and stir a few times. Now cover meat about half with stock and half with coconut milk. Quantities I don't know. It doesn't matter. Okay now salt and pepper.

So you bring it to a boil and put the jam in. This is all over hot fire. You know that. By then the onions should be done. So you put in the onions. The onions are tricky .... you want to emphasize that. You cannot let them burn... At this point you put in half the basil you got. Okay, let's say two tablespoon of chopped basil. Put at low heat with the lid on. Cook for about half hour. Then you put in bananas. Cover up and cook. Bring back to boil and then put on low again. You know that now, though.

Adjust the sweet and hot. And then you add another couple of spoons of basil, so some cooks a little and some is a little fresh. Then you cook another 10 or 15 minutes until it's ready. At the last moment you can splash a little more coconut milk on.

STEVE BOUGHTON

It was the first lead acting role for Steve Boughton, otherwise known as West Marin's singing dentist. He'd been performing for years as both musician (guitar and flute) and singer, but his lead as Albert in "Bye Bye Birdie" with the West Marin Community Chorus was a new challenge.

He played in the West Marin Community Orchestra for "King and I" and "Oklahoma." He sings with the Marin County Rock and Roll Choir and a vocal jazz quartet group called "The Accidentals."

"Jazz is harmonically more challenging. I had done mostly guitar folk stuff like Bob Dylan and Jimmy Buffet. Dylan's one of my heros. What kind of music do I like? I like it all. I'd love to sing in a rock and roll band."

Boughton's musical career began in the second grade when his teacher was teaching songs to the class. "I remember looking at the notes on the staff. It made sense to me. I sang this song and the teacher asked if my older sisters had taught it to me. I said 'no.' That was the first inkling that I had some talent in that league. In third grade, they bought me a flute. I also started singing in the church choir."

"In college I sang in the UCLA men's glee club. We toured the US, and sang in the White House. It was one of the best glee clubs in the country. In my senior year I also sang in a restaurant off campus, for a meal and all I could drink."

The choice of dentistry as a profession came about as a result of growing up in a family of health professionals (brother and father), Steve explained. "I set off in pre-med but switched to dentistry at the University of Pacific."

"I was not born with the desire to drill," he assured me with a smile. "I wanted to provide a service to people with my profession. I consider myself fortunate to be self-employed so that I can make time for other interests."

"I volunteered for a half year in Guatemala, worked in the valley, and then I worked 1-1/2 years in Oakland. I didn't like it much. So I decided to start my own practice. From a census map I figured the San Geronimo Valley had a population sufficient to support a practice, so I bought a commercial space in Lagunitas."

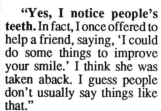

"Yes, I notice people's teeth. In fact, I once offered to help a friend, saying, 'I could do some things to improve your smile.' I think she was taken aback. I guess people don't usually say things like that."

Steve confessed he gets a kick out of being the "singing dentist." "It makes you more human, and it has helped in my business. In the office I often sing along to a tape or the radio. Sometimes I'm not even aware I do it, but people appreciate it, because it helps ease their anxieties. Singing is a great release. It's fun .... it reaches my soul."

Medallions of Pork Tenderloin

Ingredients:

tube-like pork tenderloin
1 egg, whipped
bread crumbs
olive oil
lemon

Method:

Cut the tube-like tenderloin into ice-cube-sized sections, turn on end and gently pound til flat. Gently, until thin. Then whip up some egg. Dunk the tenderloin pieces in egg, then pat into some bread crumbs and sauté in olive oil til brown (3 minutes a side). Serve with a wedge of lemon.

Breaded Chicken Breast

Ingredients:

3-4 deboned chicken breasts
2 beaten eggs
3/4 cup Progresso bread crumbs
olive oil for frying
lemon juice

Method:

Flatten chicken breasts with hands. Put a frying pan on medium high heat, and put in some olive oil.

Dunk each breast first in egg, then lay it in the bowl of bread crumbs, turning so both sides are coated, and put in the fry pan, turning when one side is lightly browned. Serve with a wedge of lemon.

JOANN STEWART

"I wanted to be a rancher all of my life," began JoAnn Stewart of Stewart Ranch in Olema. "Maybe I was imbued with the spirit of the old West, but as far back as I can remember when anyone asked what I wanted to be, that was it. I wasn't all that interested in cows as a young girl, but I was very horsey."

Stewart was born and raised on Stewart Ranch, then a Grade A dairy farm, purchased by her grandfather in 1921. After two years at Dominican College, she entered UC Davis to major in animal husbandry, then returned to the ranch, joining in the family business and starting a family of her own.

In 1964, their land was smack in the middle of the proposed Point Reyes National Seashore. Thus the land was purchased from them with a lease-back agreement allowing them to continue ranching the land.

In 1971, the dairy business was changed to a beef operation. Their pasture land, now leased from the Point Reyes National Seashore and Golden Gate National Recreation Area, includes 800 acres at the ranch, 300 acres in Bear Valley, land in Bolinas through a partnership with Niman-Schell, and land at Green Gulch, which is under a six-month permit.

Also in 1971, the family began boarding horses and breeding Morgan horses on the ranch. Today

they no longer breed and raise Morgans, but they do board 30 to 40 trail horses, and run the Stewart Ranch Horse Camp at Five Brooks, which serves as a trail-riding horse camp in the summer.

The Stewarts work in close partnership with Bill Niman and Orville Schell of Bolinas, who buy their young steers. Explained Stewart, "We have 275 mother cows, who are bred to the best Black Angus stock and calved here. When the calves are eight to 10 months old, Bill buys them from us, and we sort out the heifers and steers, weighing eaach one. You must hear them all over Bolinas, since mothers and calves are on opposites sides of the fence.

"Bill keeps them in excellent health so that each animal reaches its full potential — 1150 pounds of choice grade (organic) beef ...."

"They're my babies. I follow them all the way from conception to the meat counter at Living Foods in San Anselmo. People say good things about Niman-Schell beef. What's nice is that this is real, homegrown, West Marin beef.

"After all of this talk about beef, I'm going to give you a recipe for spare ribs,"she said with a chuckle. "We always have cole slaw and french bread with our ribs. You can use this barbecue sauce on any meat, however."

Stewart Ranch-Style Barbecue Sauce

Ingredients:

(for spare ribs or beef)
1 cup black currant jam
1/2 tsp. ginger or fresh ginger root
1 cup catsup or thick tomato juice
1/2 cup dark brown sugar
1/2 cup honey
1 Tbsp. whole allspice
1 tsp. crushed mustard seed
vinegar to taste
ribs

Method:

Sauce:
   Combine ingredients. Simmer in saucepan for 1 hour. Keep hot for two more hours. Store in a jar in the refrigerator.

BOB VOLPERT

When *Light* staffers were invited on a day-long river rafting trip by Outdoor Adventures, down the American River, no one was quite sure what we were in for.

Not to worry. Bob Volpert and his crew at Outdoor Adventures have been taking people down California and Idaho rivers for about 18 years now. They thrill and feed an average of 5,000 people a season (May 1 to September). That's about 15,000 meals, planned and cooked by the boat guides in the wilderness.

"That makes us a pretty big restaurant," said Volpert. "I think we are phenomenal cooks. It's magical what we can do out there," he teased. "There is no truth to the common myth that being outdoors makes you hungrier. Other companies make use of this ruse, but we do not. Ours is strictly skill."

Accommodating most dietary requests, the crew prepares everything from Cajun, Kosher, vegetarian dishes to steak and potatoes. The meals are a product of successful repetition .... some from suggestions by passengers. The fewer the utensils the better, so barbeques, sautés, and one-pot dishes work well. But pleasing varied palates al fresco carries innate risks, and there've been some minor snafus along the way.

"Like cakes cooked in dutch ovens that didn't work," offered Bob. "We've forgotten the food entirely and had to go back. One time all the bread for the trip washed out of the boat."

Things can quickly become precious: "On one trip we forgot the toilet paper, but the worst thing was that in trading for each roll of toilet paper, the other outfit wanted a six-pack of beer," Bob remembered with a goodnatured grimace.

Late that Saturday morning, we *Light* staffers boarded eight-person rafts, each with guide. After two hours of strenuous paddling and splashing through rapids in the chilly mountain air, serious hunger set in. At last we beached the rafts and feasted on a do-it-yourself sandwich buffet of turkey, cheese and roast beef with all the trimmings. Fruit, Oreos and M&Ms were dessert. Out on a rock, warming my toes in the sun, that lunch tasted better than anything I can remember. Boy, they sure can cook.

Here is a dinner recipe from Outdoor Adventures named after Charlie Norton, a hermit who lived on the middle fork of the Salmon River in Idaho.

Charlie Norton Chicken

Ingredients:

High quality boxed white wine (2 cups or so)
Chicken thighs, breasts, legs (24 parts)
2-1/2 cups of rice
1-1/2 lbs. mushrooms
4 cups chicken broth
1 cube butter
garlic, chopped, plenty
4 jars artichoke hearts

Method:

Sauté chicken pieces in butter, about 8 minutes a side. Add garlic, onions and continue cooking for a few minutes and throw in mushrooms and artichokes. Drink and splash wine around sauté. Add rice, cover and cook about 30 minutes. Have some more wine and hope it works. Serves 10.

ART MILLS

When Marin benefactor Beryl Buck's will was challenged, the question as to how that money should be distributed raised a heated controversy. The subsequent creation of the Marin Community Foundation provided a solution to grant-making policy.

Art Mills, resident of Point Reyes Station, with a Master's of Divinity from the San Francisco Theological Seminary, was chosen to serve as the Marin Foundation's program officer of environmental and religious projects, alongside colleague Sally Anne Wilson.

In the environmental division, program priorities include organizations which educate the public as well as efforts to enhance and conserve air, land and water resources. Four groups were given "Core Funding" — Audubon Canyon Ranch, The California Marin Mammal Center, The Marin Agricultural Land Trust, and the Marin Conservation League. Those organizations are funded for three to five years.

In the religious areas, program goals seek to bring spiritual sustenance to those who are alienated, isolated, or in crisis, with an emphasis on interdenominational understanding, in addressing human rights, ethics and social justice.

The most fun part of this job, says Mills, is "to sit down with people and explore an idea they have come to the foundation with." After reviewing the applications for funding this year(1990), Mills said he "chose from a high caliber, creative set of applications which reflect the fact that this area is nationally recognized for its environmental leadership."

"We're not doers, we're funders," said Mills. "Once a week I hike the land on on-site visits, to see the problems or places first hand."

During his five years working for the State of California in agricultural land preservation in Sacramento, Mills said, "The standout community for discussion was Marin County. The Marin Agricultural Land Trust (MALT) is the finest example of talking and working together that you'll ever see. Marin is a model community for areas like Napa, San Joaquin County, and farmers in the Stockton area. If you lose too many farms in one area, it puts pressure on the rest of the surrounding area's farmers."

One idea they're proudest of having brought to the foundation in the environmental area, said Mills, was the idea of the Baykeeper. "A guy named Michael Herz called up and said he had an idea — to launch a citizen watchdog boat to patrol several days a week, enforcing pollution control on the Bay. The idea is based on the Baykeeper of the Hudson River in New York," said Mills. "We knew it was a great idea, right away. A huge corps of volunteers and a network of private citizens now have been organized as word of the project has spread. Dr. Michael Herz is a longtime Bay Area scientist concerned with water issues. His idea came to fruition in only a year and a half."

Mills cooks, too — mostly breakfast and usually on the weekends. Here is one of his Saturday morning recipes.

Omelets with Curried Chicken

Ingredients:

1/4 cup butter or margarine
3/4 tsp. curry powder
1/2 cup sliced fresh mushrooms
3 Tbsp. sliced green onion
4 Tbsp. flour
2 cups lowfat milk
2 chicken bouillon cubes, crumbled
1/4 tsp. salt
1-1/2 cups diced cooked chicken
2 Tbsp. chopped pimento
2 Tbsp. chopped parsley
1/2 cups chopped walnuts
6 omelets

Method:

In a large skillet, melt the butter; and stir in curry powder, mushrooms, and onion. Sauté for three minutes.

Add flour. Gradually stir in milk. Add crumbled bouillon and salt; stirring constantly, until it boils and thickens. Stir in chicken, pimento, and parsley; transfer and keep warm in a double boiler while preparing omelets. Add walnuts just before serving. Spoon 1/2 cup of the sauce over each omelet.

Serves 6.

NELL MELCHER

The home of watercolorist Nell Melche,r high on the ridge, overlooks the graceful curve of Stinson Beach. On this postcard perfect day, it seemed perfectly natural for a painter to nest in this airy perch.

Bouquets of nasturtiums adorned our luncheon table in front of her drawing table where a pencil drawing-in-progress rested. "Most of my work is food related ... or wine," she said, "... and in the spring I go crazy with flowers."

As if to verify her statement, the room was filled with her highly detailed and stylized still lifes of familiar household objects: flowers, fruit, cheeses, coffee cups and half-filled glasses of wine, expertly rendered in pen and ink and brilliant watercolor washes.

From afar, her paintings have a feeling of casual homeyness. She clearly has a knack, as she says, for "combining everything but the kitchen sink and still have them work," a credit to her sense of composition, color and texture. On closer examination one becomes aware of the intricacy of her detail work, from the perfectly replicated fabric and porcelain designs, to the fine lettering on wine bottle labels — to the reflection of a wine glass in the blade of the knife laying next to it.

"I've been a painter all my life," she explained. "At four years, my father (a signpainter)

propped me up on a high stool where I watched him work. His studio was filled with cardboard sheets in a rainbow of gorgeous colors, and jars of tempera paint in every shade imaginable. Often he gave me scraps and paints to play with.

"When I first painted as an adult I did landscapes, until the 60s, when a friend asked me to paint some miniature still lifes. I had a great big kitchen with lots of windows. I would go shopping, come home, take the food out on to the counter and arrange it. It would be the inspiration for a painting."

Melcher has lived in Stinson Beach for 25 years. "Every once in a while I leave," she said, "but I always come back. Friends and the ocean bring me back. I've lived in Santa Fe, and the desert draws me as much as the ocean, but not for as long."

At the age of 46 she completed her Bachelor of Fine Arts degree at Sonoma State and has been teaching workshops and courses, as well as showing her own work both nationally and internationally since.

A prolific and dedicated artist, Melcher has had 35 one-person shows in the last 15 years, in galleries both well-known (Van Dorn's, Gumps, Bett's) and local (Anna Gardner, Stinson Beach Art Center), as well as numerous group showings.

Here is Nell Melcher's delicious, taste-tested recipe.

Summer Torta

Ingredients:

1 large onion, chopped
2 large cloves garlic, minced
6 cups sliced zucchini, yellow & crooked neck squash
1 small tomato, chopped
1/2 cup chopped mushrooms
1/4 cup olive oil
Italian herbs
pepper
1 package thawed, drained spinach
4 pieces diced cooked salami
6 eggs, beaten
1/2 tsp salt
1 cup Parmesan cheese

Method:

Cook onion, garlic, squash, tomato, and mushrooms slowly in fry ing pan with oil. Add herbs and pepper. In a large bowl, mix spinach, salami, eggs, cheese and salt with the vegetable sauté. Put in an oiled 6" x 10" pan and bake 30-40 minutes at 325 degrees.

JIM ANDERSON

Bolinas author Jim Anderson's novel, *Billarooby* is the result of five years of writing, rewriting and honing, in response to a stream of rejections from publishing houses.

During that time Anderson took a field trip to Australia, where he had grown up (the setting for this novel) to refresh his memory. His agent in New York, unwaivering in his support, continued to submit the manuscript to still more publishers. And more rejections of *Billarooby* came back — 30 in total.

"I began to get used to rejections. I liked the criticisms from the publishers. They were thoughtful and considered, often with good ideas. From them I began a series of rewrites — eight in all — against the advice of my agent who thought it was good as it was. But with each rewrite, the book got better and better, tighter and shorter."

Discouraged, and out of money, Anderson submitted a chapter of the book to the Marin Arts Council, and went to work at the Bolinas People's Store. Two weeks later, he got the call from the Arts Council. They were so impressed with his work that they wanted to give him not the $5,000 he'd asked for, but $10,000 to finish his novel.

"When the Arts Council grant came through I was tremendously encouraged," said Anderson. "I bought myself an IBM computer, and with a burst of enthusiasm, sat down, did the last revision, and sent it off to my agent. He was delighted and sent it off to two more publishers. Ticknor and Fields accepted it."

"*Billarooby* is based on authentic events and places in my childhood, but it is a story. There was a drought, my father did have a large garden, and we lived near a Japanese prisoner of war camp. But I was only six when the massacre occurred in the war camp.

"The book is about rejection and intimate relationships such as father-son. In the book I solve it as I never did in real life. It is strong, heartfelt. My sisters find it so emotionally distressing they won't read the book."

With the publication of *Billarooby* there've been offers for movie rights, interviews, and tours. But Anderson is not starry eyed with success. He said, "I'm looking forward to the tours (of London and Australia) but I don't particularly enjoy the publicity. I'm shy in front of a camera. I'm not interested in working on the screeplay. It's extremely cinematic, but I've been with *Billarooby* for five years. I'm interested in only one thing: writing my new book. I don't have many stories in me, but I do have three or four. The next one is set in Ghana, West Africa."

"At one time during my outback, Australian childhood, we ate an awful lot of rabbit. We certainly got heartily sick of it. Our mother was always devising new ways of cooking it. Sauteed rabbit, roast rabbit, fricasee of rabbit, left over rabbit, ground up and turned into rissoles, and one memorable summer, when a friend of the family sent us a case of cherries on the train, we had a Rabbit Cherry Pie. My mother's original recipe has long since disappeared, but I have on occasion attempted a version. Here it is.

Rabbit Cherry Pie

Ingredients:

1 pre-baked pie shell
1 rabbit, cut in pieces
seasoned flour
several cloves garlic chopped
1 medium onion
handful mushrooms
olive oil
1-1/2 cups dry red wine
1 tsp. balsamic vinegar
ground black pepper
1 Tbsp. cornstarch
2 cups pitted black cherries
1/2 cup boiling water
1 Tbsp. sugar
dash of Kirsch liqueur

Method:

First, catch your rabbit, in this country and these days, probably at the butcher's counter. Cut poor beast into pieces and dredge with flour. Sauté garlic, onion and mushrooms to taste, in olive oil. I am always generous with the garlic. Remove garlic, onion and mushrooms from oil, and brown the rabbit. Add wine, vinegar and sprinkle liberally with ground black pepper. Cover the skillet and simmer until the meat is very tender, probably an hour or so. Return the garlic, onion and mushrooms to the covered skillet 15 minutes or so before the rabbit is done. If necessary, thicken the sauce with a little cornstarch, or reduce it before hand by leaving off the lid.

Pit 2 cups cherries, drop into 1/2 cup boiling water. Reduce heat and simmer until nearly tender. Add sugar and Kirsch. Cook a few more minutes.

Strip the cooked rabbit from the bones. Place the meat and cherries in the pie shell. Pour on top both the meat sauce and the cherry sauce. Cover with pre-baked pie topping and heat in the oven at 300 degrees until the top is light brown and the contents thoroughly hot.

JANET KJELMYR AND GEOFF GEUPEL

"Birds help forecast environment's health," read the headline in the *Marin Independent Journal*. The occasion was the 25th anniversary of the Point Reyes Bird Observatory. Geoff Geupel and Janet Kjelmyr have worked with the Observatory's growing program for six years, studying birds and marine mammal life here and in Antarctica.

For four years, each October, Kjelmyr and Geupel left their home in Bolinas for a six-month stay in a tiny hut on Admiralty Bay in Antarctica. The summer breeding season for three species of penguins has been the focus of their attention and research. But summer in Antarctica is as likely to be sunny and 40 degrees as it is a sub-freezing blizzard.

"It takes about a month to adjust to life down there," said Geupel. "You slow way down, no radio, no TV."

"It means that you are able to concentrate without interruption," added Kjelmyr. "And there's plenty of daylight since the sun sets at midnight for only two hours."

Kjelmyr was out in the field every day, for at least eight hours, watching the nests and behavior of a rookery of about 18,000 penguins,

Adelies, Gentoos and Chinstraps. They take four to five years to mature, so she recognizes many from past years — most are banded for identification. But half of the population doesn't return, perhaps due to food shortages and severe winters. Nobody knows exactly where the penguins go in the winter, since severe weather conditions make tracking them difficult.

"Our hut is located only 50 yards from shore and right on the penguins' path to their nesting places in the rocks," described Kjelmyr. ".They have loyal mates, and they have divorces and confusion. They make nests with rocks, and steal the rocks from each other. While one is stealing from one, another steals hers (or his). Both sexes sit on the nest. When it snows, you can find the penguins by looking down deep holes in the snow. They sit on their nests with their beaks raised for air."

It might get unbearably lonely were it not for the other bases located nearby. Eighteen different countries have research bases in Antarctica. Kjelmyr and Geupel exchange visits with the Brazilian, Polish, and Russian bases, which happen to be nearest them. "It's kind of an international community, and the harsh environment and isolation bring people together," said Kjelmar. "A new face becomes a very exciting event, even if you can't speak the language, so people visit and share food together often.

"Our food arrives in huge boxes, dumped by a helicopter on the shore next to all the seals and penguins. It's military-issue food, and it's often very funny what they supply the two of us with," said Geupel. "They gave us cases of 'Stay-puff' marshmallows, four cases of Cheeze Whiz, cases of Cocoa Puffs in little boxes, and No. 10 cans of fruit cocktail. One year we had no spices, so, sure enough, the next year we were supplied with garlic powder and black pepper *by the case*. We gave the salad dressing to the Poles, since we had no salad to put it on. They put it on everything — even drank it straight from the jar."

Admiralty Bay Feijoada

When the holidays come around, most of the nationalities celebrate Christmas, but the American tradition of Thanksgiving baffled the Poles and Brazilians. "It was difficult for them to grasp the significance of Thanksgiving and turkeys .... We'd begin describing about the Indians and Pilgrims and they'd say 'We thought you killed all the Indians,' " said Kjelmar with a shrug.

Here's a Brazilian-Polish recipe with a dash of Caribbean influence, Suzie's Hot Sauce, enjoyed by Kjelmyr and Geupel and their fellow scientists in Antarctica.

Ingredients:

2 cups black beans (soaked 12 hours)
1 large onion, chopped
Polish Kielbasa (pork sausage)
2-3 cloves garlic, minced
Suzie's Caribbean Hot Sauce, to taste
(or your favorite)

Method:

Rinse, cover and boil beans for 2-3 hours. Sauté onions and garlic. Crumble in sausage. Splash with hot sauce. Add to beans, stir. Serve alone or over rice.

MEXICAN ENTRÉES

DANIEL RILLEAU

This professional chef, Daniel Rilleau, caught and cooked his first fish in Provincetown, Massachusetts, on the tip of Cape Cod. Known once as "Helltown" for its inhabitation by outlaws and smugglers, this was the rugged birthplace of our nation's commercial fishing industry.

"It was [and is] a resort town, and if you lived there, you either fished or worked in a restaurant," explained Rilleau. "I had no formal training. I cooked for survival. But business is seasonal. I came out here [to the West Coast] looking for a year-round economy."

He found West Marin to be more like Provincetown than any place he'd ever been, both geographically and in preferences of the palate. Coast to coast, oysters seem to be universally loved; appreciated for their enhancement of the dinner hour and credited for all things amorous after that.

Cape Codders sing praises to the Wellfleet oyster, raw and chilled naked on the half shell with a sqeeze of lemon and drop of Tabasco. We lust for the Pacific oyster, introduced in the 1920s, after the native Olympia oyster was wiped out during the Gold Rush days.

Local oysterman also tease us with the French Belon and Japanese Kumamoto, splashed with fresh, lime-cilantro sauce. New Englanders boast their haddock, striped bass, and swordfish; we crave salmon, halibut and snapper.

"People here really know their fish," Rilleau said. "You know when people order their salmon *rare,* they're pretty particular about it. I never had an order for rare fish on the East coast."

In his 15 years of restaurant work, Rilleau has served Italian, French (locally at Le Camembert), New England, California (Carlos O'Brien's,) Nouvelle, Mexican (Old Mexico Grill, Santa Fe) and Tex Mex cuisine in kitchens which served up to 450 dinners nightly (Ciro & Sals, Provincetown).

Rilleau now cooks at the Inverness Inn, at the end of town. Dinners at the Inn emphasize local, fresh seafood, although Rilleau is just as happy to cook Mexican entrees. He is happily married, with a young son named Jesse. Fatherhood becomes him, and he's anxious to have another one, he said with a smile.

Rilleau began to describe a dinner he had prepared for his neighbors: a unique Mexican feast, unlike anything you will ever find in a Mexican restaurant, he assured me. Here are recipes to make the whole dinner.

An Elegant Mexican Dinner

Calabacitas (Squash)
Serves 4

Ingredients:

3/4 cup heavy cream
2 cups corn (fresh)
2 cups diced zucchini
1 cup diced skinned, seeded tomato
1 tsp. diced garlic
1 tsp. cinnamon
4 Tbsp. olive oil
salt & pepper to taste

Method:

In a large, deep skillet, bring oil to high heat. Add corn and zucchini. Stir frequently for 2-3 minutes. Add garlic, then diced tomato. Finally add cream and cinnamon (still over high heat) until cream reduces enough to thicken the entire mixture. Add salt and pepper. Serve with rice, and filet mignon (below).

Chipotle Sauce
(Serve over beef filets grilled on Mesquite coals)

Ingredients:

1/4 cup diced onion
2 tsp. minced garlic
1/4 cup pureed canned tomatillos
3 Tbsp. canned Chipotle chiles in Adobo sauce
1/4 cup heavy cream
2 Tbsp. olive oil

Method:

Sauté onion and garlic in saucepan for several minutes. Add tomatillos and Chipotle chiles and simmer for 5 minutes. Purée in blender until smooth. Return to saucepan and add heavy cream. Stir thoroughly.

Rice with Cilantro

Ingredients:

1 cup converted rice
2 cups chicken stock or broth
1/2 cup unseasoned canned tomato sauce
1/4 cup diced onion
1/4 cup chopped cilantro
1 Tbsp. olive oil

Method:

Combine chicken stock with tomato sauce and mix thoroughly. Bring oil to high heat in sauce pan, add onion and rice — stir coating rice with oil. Add chicken stock-tomato mixture, then chopped cilantro. Stir thoroughly with a fork, keep on high heat until you reach a boil, lower heat and cover until all liquid is absorbed, about 20 minutes.

DAVE DESANTE

The study of bird populations is the lifelong work of Dave DeSante of Inverness. As he pointed out the coloration, feathering and migration patterns of 10 species of sparrows at his home feeder, he explained why.

Changes in bird populations throughout the world are very real indicators of environmental changes which eventually affect us all. "The changes bird populations will be facing in the next 20 years are global environmental changes," said DeSante. "The three big ones are global warming, changes in gross habitat (deforestation of rainforests) and pollution (acid rain, chloroflourocarbons and low-level radiation). These changes know no boundaries. They aren't limited to any geographical area, so you can see the importance of large data sets — a global approach to monitoring these changes."

To this end DeSante has created an organization which is dedicated to a global approach toward research and information dissemination on the subject of changes in bird populations. It's called "The Institute for Bird Populations."

The plan consists of five projects: 1) An annual scientific journal of documented research; 2) a Monitoring Avian Productivity project of cooperative bird banding in North America; 3) The Subalpine Avian Ecology/Global Climate Project — a longterm research project (begun in 1977) studying the effects of global warming; 4) the Global

Environment Education Project; and 5) the Bird Populations newsletter.

For one guy with a computer in a little cabin in West Marin, this would seem a monumental task. But DeSante has a systematic approach to his goals. He's self-published two books on North American birds under the name Slate Creek Press, one documenting useful information on determining age and sex of birds for banders, the other, a complete list of all the birds in North America, illustrated by Keith Hansen and Tony Bennett.

Even at age 10, DeSante recalled, "I made several books of drawings of birds in the area I lived in Ohio." But as he was growing up, it occurred to no one that one could make a living on the study of birds. So he studied Metallurgical Engineering at Stanford, obtaining first a bachelor's degree and then a master's, until "my graduate work got in the way of birdwatching. I was fascinated by the (then) recent discovery of lost warblers from the East Coast. So I switched to the Biology Department at Stanford, I randomly chose the name 'Peter Raven' from the faculty list. As it turned out Raven is a brilliant defender of the tropical rainforests. I chose the only person, very likely, who would listen to my ideas. We made friends instantly.... I ended up doing my doctoral research on 'Vagrant Warblers on the Farallones,' " said DeSante.

Chili Rellenos

Ingredients:

6 large whole green canned chilis
sliced jack cheese
4 eggs, yolks separated from whites
1/4 cup organic (please) whole wheat flour
butter or oil to grease skillet

Method:

Slice chilis lengthwise to open. Place a slice of jack cheese inside chili. Separate egg yolks from whites. Beat whites until stiff, fold in the yolks, sprinkle flour in to make a fluffy batter. Lightly grease a skillet, put some batter on the griddle, set chile in it, cover with more batter. When browned, flip over to cook other side. Serve hot with home-made salsa.

MICHELE JIMENEZ

In the old days, the job of lighthouse keeper on Point Reyes would quite possibly drive one crazy. It was a lonely, desolate place to be. One keeper who went bonkers had to be taken away. Winds have been clocked at 133 mph on the point, and dense fog has been known to roll in like a visit from in-laws: long days stretching into weeks.

The keepers of the light couldn't leave. On six-hour shifts, they tended the gas lantern each night (they were nicknamed "wickies") and shoveled coal to keep the fog horn sounding night and day, polishing and cranking the brass housings and lenses so that passing ships would avoid the treacherous rocks below.

Michele Jimenez, an interpretive ranger and tour guide at the Lighthouse, is free from such menial duties. Her job is to teach and remind us of the history and nature around us. She considers herself the link between the park and the people, often explaining conservation and environmental issues to the public.

It's not uncommon for her to talk to 1,000 people on a weekend during the whale-watching season.

As she led a group of us down the 300 steps to the Lighthouse, she explained, "Most lighthouses are built as high as possible, but around here we have 'high fog,' so the light is more effective at a lower level."This day the weather was unuusual — calm and hot and sunny. Michele said that it is more often very foggy and cold, or very windy, which is why she recommends warm clothing for a visit to the lighhouse.

The Park Service has kept the original Fresnel light in working condition since 1975 when the system was fully automated. The light still works exactly the way it did for 105 years; surviving the 1906 earthquake with damage repaired in time for the evening mists. It's a beautiful polished brass set of gears inside a wood and glass case. On top of this sits 3,000 pounds of cut-glass prisms (the Fresnel lens), which rotate on small brass "chariot wheels" on the housing.

Michele cranked the brass housing which raises a 175-pound counterweight, which in turn rotates the lens. The light from a gas lantern is refracted by this lens into 24 separate beams. A clock-like series of gears keeps it rotating at a slow, steady rate, making the flash appear every five seconds.

This is a recipe often enjoyed by Michele and her fellow rangers, at the lighthouse station in Point Reyes.

Lighthouse Enchiladas

Ingredients:

Sauce:
1/4 cup flour
1/4 cup chili powder
1-32 oz. can tomato sauce
1/4 cup cocoa

Filling:
1 medium onion, diced
1/2 bunch spinach, chopped
1-1/2 lb. ground turkey/beef
1 small can chopped olives
1 Tbsp. ground cumin
1 Tbsp. garlic powder
salt and pepper to taste
1 dozen corn tortillas
1-1/2 lb. jack cheese

Method:

Sauce:
Brown slightly flour and chili powder in dry pan. Add tomato sauce, 1/4 cup cocoa. Stir occasionally. Set aside.

Filling:
Brown turkey or beef, drain excess fat. Add diced onion, sautéeing until clear. Add olives, cumin and garlic and stir. Stir in chopped spinach, cooking until it goes limp. Add salt and pepper to taste.

Slightly warm one dozen corn tortillas. Dip each into sauce, then place on a plate. Spoon filling mixture into center of tortilla. Top with shredded cheese. Put some of the sauce on the bottom of an oblong, glass baking dish. Roll and place tortillas in dish. Top enchiladas with remaining sauce and cheese. Cover and bake at 350 degrees for 30 minutes. Serve hot.

MIKE MESZAROS

Next to the softly babbling creek behind the Inverness Fire House, fire chief Mike Mezaros sat down on the fire hose drying rack and told of first love, sailing, and his career as a fire fighter. In this idyllic green setting, it was hard to imagine any danger of fire.

His family moved to Inverness when Mike was nine years old. "My father stuck me in a sailing program down at the yacht club. I had this fear of capsizing. So after two years of sailing gingerly, I managed my first capsize .... Of course it was right in front of everyone at the the dock, by the interfloat at the yacht club."

When Mike turned 18, he and a friend volunteered as firefighters "so we could drive the fire trucks." After acquiring a degree in oceanography and biology, Meszaros came back to Inverness to stay, becoming fire chief in 1981, just in time for the 1982 floods.

"It was more than an initiation," he said. "The flood was a turning point for the department as well. All of a sudden we were recognized. Our emergency plan to provide food and shelter and medical care was used for a while as a model for other communities. This job is still a 24-hour responsibility, but I do take time to get out on the water."

When the wind is up, Mike's often windsurfing on Tomales Bay. "Board sailing isn't

an easy sport to take up," Meszaros confessed. "It's a struggle just to stay on the board at first. It takes upper body strength and stamina. I chuckle at people starting out ... You fall off a whole lot ... I know. But once you get the basics down, and are able to stay on, tack and jibe, then most people acquire a harness hooked to the boom. Properly adjusted, it takes the strain off your arms and you can go a long time. Sometimes I go out for two or three hours at a time."

The radio inside the fire house interrupted our conversation and we strained to hear. "County's broken its first wildland fire." Meszaros said with surprise. Over the radio came more details. "Mt. Tam ... strong east wind... moving toward structure ... three engines and a helicopter... heavy traffic."

This was beginning to get exciting. I wrote furiously as Mike explained in detail the complex maneuverings of equipment around the county, and quite a bit of information about the spreading of fire on Mt. Tam. Suddenly he stopped and laughed. "Scratch all that," he said. "That was a simulation. We must have missed the first part."

Here is Mike Meszaros's recipe for Baja Beans, created on one of his annual camping treks to Cabo Pulmo, Mexico, for his appreciative and hungry board-sailing companions.

Mike Meszaros's Baja Beans

Ingredients:

Canned kidney or pink beans (or you can cook them yourself)
Chorizo, crumbled or finely chopped bacon
1 Tbsp. oil or bacon/chorizo rendering
1 chopped onion
2-3 cloves garlic, chopped
Monterey jack cheese
Optional additions:
hot sauce
1 hot chili (chipotle)
squirt of lime juice
dash of tequila
crumbled Mexican chocolate

Method:

Sauté crumbled chorizo, or finely chopped bacon in a frying pan. Add onions and garlic to that. Mash the beans with liquid into the onions. Add Monterey Jack cheese, and then, to taste; hot sauce, chilis, lime juice, tequila, Mexican chocolate .... I prefer them the second day .... for breakfast. And I like them "chinitos" (fried until crisp).

ERNEST AND INGRID NOYES

Musicians and songwriters Ernest and Ingrid Noyes, known as "Noyes and More Noyes," promote music in Tomales — monthly music nights at their home and a concert series Saturday evenings in the summer. "When people come together to play music, some come with instruments you didn't even known they had," said Ingrid, who plays piano, guitar, banjo. Ernest plays all of those plus the mandolin.

"What kind of music do we play?" Ingrid and Ernest glanced at each other. "It's bluegrass, oldtime, country; some people call our music folk, or Appalachian mountain music, and some of it is 20s and 30s style," said Ernest. Ingrid added, "We write our own music, too, which is kind of contemporary folk." They were having trouble describing their sound; as Laurie Anderson once said: "Talking about music is like dancing about architecture."

Ingrid expressed her disillusionment with AM radio music of today. "I might be old-fashioned, but I grew up in the 60s and I can't help believing that you need a melody, some rhythm and good lyrics to call it music."

The Noyeses have performed at Dance Palace Talent Shows, Preschool fundraisers, the Petaluma Songwriters Showcase and for a woman's 91st birthday party in Nevada City. They did a radio show for KSRO AM and belong to the Folk Music Societies in San Francisco and Sonoma.

"One reaction we often get is: 'I thought this kind of music was gone. You guys are great,' " noted Ingrid. "People always ask about the instruments. Often they've never seen a banjo or a mandolin .... Sometimes I'll go to a concert, and I'll hear drums but there's no drummer. I'll hear a bass, and it's really a synthesizer. Bands are now computerized, and their players are technicians. I miss the soul and life of real people playing music."

Ingrid and Ernest met on the Green Tortoise, a kind of underground bus line which provides inexpensive fares, campground accommodations, and lots of fun for its riders. Ingrid and Ernest were the drivers for this trip, bound for the Mardi Gras. The two of them ended up entertaining the travellers — and each other — playing music each night.

Life in Tomales is "natural, like breathing," said Ernest. "We are fairly self-sufficient, have a low rent, no expensive habits, and we camp on our vacations. Things are changing, but we'd rather have time to be with each other and our kid than have other things."

Here is a Green Tortoise recipe developed especially for cooking enchiladas on a camp stove, instead of the oven as is usually done. (Green Tortoise kitchens include stoves, but not ovens).

Stacked Enchiladas

Ingredients:

Enchilada Sauce (your favorite)
1 package corn tortillas

Filling: Choose from
spicy refried beans
rice
grated jack cheese
chopped olives
chopped onions
cilantro, chopped finely
sautéed beef (optional)

Method:

Dunk tortillas in sauce, one at a time, and cover bottom of skillet. Spread some beans, then rice, cheese, olives, onions, cilantro and beef. Then pour more sauce, then more tortillas, filling, continue, finishing up with grated cheese on the top. Cover and put on lowest possible heat. Simmer until cheese melts and bubbles. Serve with sour cream and a green salad.

SKIP SCHWARTZ

Audubon Canyon Ranch is one of the world's major nesting areas of the Great Blue Heron and the Great Egret. The heron nesting season begins in February, and the Egrets (the majority of the birds) begin in late March. You can see the birds in the redwood tree-tops even from Highway 1 along the Bolinas Lagoon outside of Stinson Beach. A visit inside to Audubon Canyon Ranch's permanent exhibit will tell you how it all came about. It's a heroic story with pictures, too.

Skip Schwartz, the general manager of the ranch, gave me a personal introduction to the ranch. The area very nearly did not become a wildlife sanctuary. In 1967, the entire Bolinas Lagoon and surrounding hillside was slated for commercial development — yach clubs, marinas, condominiums. Due to the efforts of a few folks from the Marin Audubon Society, the land was bought and protected as a 100-acre natural bird sanctuary.

"Have you ever looked into a nest of white Egret chicks from the hillside?" asked Schwartz, shaking his head. "To see them fly for the first time is.... an epiphanal natural experience. It cuts through political and social barriers."

Schwartz came to the ranch with his wife, about the time of the 1971 "great oil spill" in the Bolinas Lagoon, and took a 22-day docent train-ing course (now a national model of docent training). They decided to stay and work on the project of creating an environmental sanctuary and educational workplace, eventually moving into the big white "New England cracker box" house on the grounds. They raised three children on the ranch. Schwartz also served as an Emergency Medical Technician with the Bolinas Fire Department for 12 years.

Walking up one of the loop trails, Schwartz expressed his concerns with the environmental movement. "I'm concerned that the environment isn't relevant enough [to under-developed countries]. It sometimes comes down to clean water or a job. People shouldn't have to make that choice. ... It's important for developed countries like ours to find out what's relevant to other cultures. We're working on a multi-cultural training program right now."

A Jewish-Mexican cowboy raised in West Texas, Skip's mother insisted, "If your nose doesn't run and your eyes don't water, it's not hot enough." Skip urges, "Be creative. Eat salsa with whatever you like .... turkey and cranberries, even. Food is just a good excuse to eat salsa."

Skip's Salsa

Ingredients:
(Makes 2 quarts, a full blender)

2-3 large fresh garden tomatoes
4 tomatillos, quartered and husked
2 red bell peppers, chopped
1/2 medium yellow onion, chopped very fine
fresh garlic, hand crushed and chopped
1-2 stalks celery, destrung and chopped
fresh cilantro leaves, chopped with no stems
6-8 jalapeno peppers, skinned & chopped (see directions)
Hungarian hot paprika
1 tsp. brown sugar

Method:

To skin jalapenos, roast by rolling around in hot frying pan til outside is scorched black. Put in a towel to sit and steam. The clear peel comes off easily with a knife, but it's good to keep some of the charred flesh for flavor. Don't touch eyes or skin after handling jalapenos. The same thing can be done with red peppers. Remove all seeds. A good salsa never has seeds in it.

Chop and prepare onion, bell peppers, tomatoes, jalapenos, celery, tomatillos, cilantro leaves and garlic, crushing the garlic to release flavor. Place these ingredients in blender beginning with the tomatoes (the bulk of the ingredients) or if chopped very fine, a blender's not necessary. Add paprika and brown sugar. Pulse it now and then so it's chunky, pushing the top stuff to the bottom, but not pushing the spoon into the blades when they're on, or you get Skip's salsa on the ceiling. Let it sit a while; the flavors need to marry. The red peppers give it a good color. The paprika, a rich look.

ALICIA CÉJA

This face is familiar to the Mexican community and to those West Marin diners who recall the delicious Mexican meals served at Mi Casa, on main street in Pt. Reyes Station. Alicia Céja and her daughter, also Alicia, cooked and served those Mexican meals with aplomb.

Mrs. Céja misses the restaurant. "It's hard work, being in the restaurant business. I would work 12- to 14-hour days. But I have to work anyway, and I enjoyed it. I do it for myself. ...Rich? No the restaurant business will not make me rich. But I like it. Now I wait for the right place [for a new restaurant]."

So while the Céjas look for a new place, I decided to try to convince Mrs. Céja to divulge her recipe for the rich, spicy-chocolate chicken molé. What cookbook would be complete without this inclusion? Mrs. Céja, in a good-natured refusal, had earlier said, "Why would anyone want to make this? It would take too long, and it is very difficult to do from scratch." With a shrug and a laugh, she said, "Just go to the market and get a jar of molé sauce and put it on the chicken. It is much easier."

My Spanish being what it is, even this simple communication took some time. But I persisted. I pleaded with her, wrote to her, even followed her to her job to convince her of the urgency of my request. I said I'd take dictation, bring a translator, even accept it written in Spanish. She gave in.

She still thinks making this from scratch is silly. But she patiently explained every step. She even brought out the ingredients, so I could see for myself what the packages of Mexican chiles, dried ginger, chocolate and sesame seeds look like. She says you can find these Mexican specialty items at Lucky's, in Petaluma. With help in translation by daughter Alicia, we managed to recreate the recipe. Molé sauce is not for dieters. It is rich, gooey and sublime.

Here I include the recipe in English, but you will find on the following pages, a version in Spanish, with instructions translated by Carolyn Maas, an intern at *The Point Reyes Light*.

We thought you might enjoy Point Reyes Station's publisher Michael Sykes's Marguerita recipe while you are cooking.

ChickenMolé

Ingredients:

1 chicken, cut into parts
1/2 lb. chiles anchos
4 oz. chilacate (or black chili, "chile negro")
4 oz. chile pasilla
4 oz. whole almonds
4 oz. peanuts
4 oz. walnuts
4 oz. white sesame seeds
2 oz. dried cilantro
5-6 tomatoes chopped
1 tortilla
Seeds from the chiles
1 head garlic, peeled, sliced
4 dozen black peppercorns
1 dozen cloves
1 piece dried Mexican ginger
1 chunk or tablet of Mexican Chocolate
1-1/2 lb. pork rind (fat)
lard for frying

Method:

A note on these chiles: They often come in 3 ounce packages, are long, black, slightly soft, and are not necessarily hot. It depends on the chile.

With the three kinds of chiles, remove stems, split open and remove seeds, saving them for later. Over medium heat, in some of the lard, fry the chiles, with the almonds, peanuts and walnuts and tortilla (torn up) until they are slightly toasted. Do not burn them.

In a dry fry pan, lightly toast the white sesame seeds, dried cilantro, seeds from chiles and garlic slices.

Put both mixtures into a blender, adding just enough water or chicken stock to moisten, and grind it, adding tomatoes, peppercorns, cloves, and ginger. You can also add chocolate, but it dissolves as well later in the chicken stock. Strain this mixture through a sieve. It will be thick and black.

Put chicken pieces in a deep casserole pot, adding enough water to just cover them. Boil the chicken for 1/2 hour. (In Mexico, Alicia says, chickens take a lot longer to cook.) Add dark mixture to the chicken and stir. Serve this over rice.

Molé Poblano

Ingredientes:

1 pollo, dividido en secciones
1/2 libra chiles anchos
4 onzas chilacate (chile negro)
4 onzas chile pasilla
4 onzas almendras limpias (enteras)
4 onzas cacahuates
4 onzas nueces de nogal
4 onzas ajonjoli dorados en comal
   (pepitas blancas de sesame)
2 onzas cilantro seco
5 or 6 tomates medianes casidos, cortados en cubos
1 tortilla dorada en manteca
semillas de los chiles
1 diente de ajo, descortezado y rebanado (cortado)
1 cabeza de ajo asada y molida
4 docenas de pimienteros negros
1 docenas de clavos
un pedazo de jengibre méjicano seco
1 Tablilla de chocolate méjicano
1-1/2 libra grasa de cerdo
   (lonja de puerco en pedacitos)
manteca de puerco para freír

Method:

Nota con respeto a los chiles: suelen estan en paquetes de 3 onzas, son largso, negros, un poquito suave y todos noson picantes — depende del chile.

Con los tres tipos de chiles, quite Ud. los pendúculos, abre y quita las pepitas (semillas) y quarde para después. Freía los chiles en parte del lardo sobre calor mediano, con las almendras cacahuates y nueces y tortilla (pongala hacia arriba) hasta estan un poquito tostados. No los queme. En un sartén seco, tuesta un poquito las pepitas blancas, des sesame, el cilantro seco, las pepitas de los chiles y rebanadas del ajol.

Meta los dos mezclas en un una máquina para entremezclar los ingredientes. Añade solamente bastante aqua para mojarla y muela toda. Añade tomates, pimenteros, clavos y jengibre. Se puede añadir chocolate también, pero el se disuelve también en el caldo de pollo. Cuelela a través un tamiz. Estará negro y denso.

Meta los secciones de pollo en una olla honda y añade bastante aqua solamenta para taparlos. Hierva el pollo para media hora. (En Mexico, dice Alica, los pollos requiren más tiempo para quisarse.) Sirva: sobre arroz.

Michael Sykes's Margueritas En Las Rocas

Ingredients:

several good fresh juicy limes
good clear Jose Cuerva white Tequila
Hiram Walker Triple Sec
sea salt

Method:

Mood and setting are crucial to the appreciation of this recipe. Approach tequila with respect. It comes from a cactus plant.

Secret:

Have everything ice cold in the freezer; your glasses and the pitcher you mix them up in.

Squeeze limes until you have a half cup of lime juice.

Take your pitcher out of the freezer and strain into the pitcher your lime juice, a half cup Triple Sec, and 1 cup Tequila. Put it back into the freezer.

Then take glasses out of the freezer. Rub the riim of each one with a squeezed lime. Dip glass rims into sea salt. Then put ice cubes in a glass. Take pitcher out. Give it a stir. Pour into the glass sot that it comes up to the salted rim. If it is very cold, a vapor forms over the surface.

Take your first sip of this delightful concoction.

CARLOS & ROSA GAMEZ

Mastery of the English language is the first thing on the minds of Carlos and Rosa Gamez of Inverness Park. That is, after the upbringing of their two daughters, Yanami and Leslie, who are fast becoming bilingual on their own.

"I can understand everything that you say," explained Carlos, "but it's more difficult to speak it." And with that he told me the story of how he and Rosa came from Mexico to live in West Marin.

A Marine Biology student in Mexico's La Autonoma de Sinaloa, Carlos was paid a scholarship of 400 pesos a month to study for five and a half years. During those years he met Rosa. She smiled as he eagerly told the story of their romance.

"A friend asked me to go on the ferry to Baja. I said I could not go, I had no money, but the friend offered me 1,000 pesos to go with him because he didn't want to go alone. I met Rosa on the ferry. I told my friend I like that girl. He said he did too. I got very angry and said, 'I saw her first.' But he was joking. Rosa was only 15 years old and she was traveling with her mother. They were buying goods to sell in La Paz.

"The trip from Mazatlan takes 12 hours and we danced all night. I followed Rosa and her mother on their shopping the next day. The return trip took 24 hours, so by then I had taken down her telephone and address."

"When I first went to visit her, her mother said 'She is tired, sleeping.' She was jealous. Rosa was so young. But later she was friendly. I visited every 15 days until I was out of school. We arranged for Rosa to finish her secondary school in Mazatlan."

In the meantime, Carlos went to find work. He went to Mexico City, Colima, Baja. "In one big office, the guy joked with me: 'We have lots of jobs, but no money.'" Carlos went to work with his brother, in a typewriter repair shop, but the salary was very low. He then worked on a carpentry crew in Tijuana on the construction of Hotel Fiesta America.

They came to live in Los Angeles in 1983, then moved to Point Reyes Station to join Carlos's brother, who works at Toby's Feed Barn. They fell in love with West Marin. Carlos found work at the Station House Cafe, gardening on off days. Rosa works at Johnson's Oysters.

Carlos enthused, "People say, why don't *you* work at Johnson's, since I specialized (in school) in oysters. You see, in Mexico you must work for one year of social services in order to graduate, and I worked for oyster fishermen. But, I make more money with what I do."

Rosa went to the kitchen and emerged with a large wrapped crab which she insisted I take home. She then gave me this delicious recipe.

Mexican Crab Salad

Ingredients:

1 large tomato, chopped
1 avocado, chopped
1 onion, chopped
1 serrano pepper, to taste
bunch of cilantro, chopped finely
lemon juice
salt

Method:

Boil the crab for 5 minutes in a large pot. Allow it to cool until you can handle it. Crack and take out meat. Mix the crab meat with tomatoes, avocados, onion, pepper, cilantro, lemon juice and salt. Chill in the refrigerator and serve on a bed of lettuce or with crackers.

RICK KLEIN

Stepping into the stucco blue and white interior of the new Casa del Mar Bed and Breakfast was akin to stumbling on a villa in Monaco, but this is Stinson Beach. Innkeeper Rick Klein greeted me with a hot cup of coffee and colorful plate of fruit and cakes.

Casa del Mar, a work of art itself, also serves as a gallery for an eclectic choice of art work — the playful, brilliant colors of work by Gary Stephens, Billy Rose, and many other Marin painters. Each piece is lit with low-voltage spots, as are small flower bouquets and sculptures.

"I didn't cut any corners, and it cost a fortune," Klein confessed with exhausted pride. For two and a half years since he purchased the house, renovation and reconstruction have been his exclusive obsession. Now he is trying innkeeping, and it suits him well.

"It's on-the-job training. I've learned how to clean bathrooms in half the time and how far the bed sheet should turn over ... I never knew anything about this — I lived on a fishing boat." He stopped and then broke into a hearty laugh. His experiences as a commercial fisherman, lawyer, contractor, and restaurateur have all helped, but he has vigorously sought help from seminars, books, other innkeepers, gardeners, bakers, friends and business people.

Each of the four upstairs bedrooms is named for the hand-painted ceramic design (by Brenda Rose) in the private, low-flow shower that adjoins the room: shells, passion flowers, hummingbirds and herons. A white, shell-shaped sink adorns each bathroom.

Each queen-sized bed is dressed in 100-percent cotton hand-printed duvets and sheets so fresh and clean you can smell the package they came from. A mountain of plump pillows covers half the bed.

The brass-hinged doors of each bedroom open out onto private verandas. In the back, one can gaze directly up at Mount Tamalpais: flocks of birds dance against the background of mists and greenery. The front overlooks extensive gardens, first created in the 1930s, bearing unique varieties of plants from cactus to rose, which Klein's botanist friends are still discovering. Paths wander and circumscribe the tall stucco house. The surf on Stinson Beach keeps time in the background.

The breakfast main course at Casa del Mar is always accompanied by fresh fruit, granola, yogurt and a fresh baked pastry or cake item. Here is a breakfast favorite from Rick Klein's Mediterranean kitchen.

Black Bean Pancakes, Huevos Rancheros & Salsa

Black Bean Pancakes

Ingredients:

1 cup cooked black beans
1/4 cup water
2 Tbsp. dry sherry
2 beaten eggs
1/4 cup minced scallions,
  (save green part for garnish)
1 clove garlic, peeled and crushed
2 Tbsp. toasted sesame seeds
2 Tbsp. sesame oil
2 Tbsp. minced gingerroot
12 drops Tabasco sauce
3/4 tsp. salt
3 Tbsp. all-purpose flour
vegetable oil to grease skillet

Method:

Process or blend 1/2 beans with water and sherry until smooth. Add eggs, processing til blended. Pour into a bowl. Stir in the remaining beans, scallions, garlic, sesame seeds, oil, gingerroot, Tabasco and salt. Sprinkle the flour onto the mixture, one tablespoon at a time, beating it with a fork until blended.

Turn oven to warm. Lightly grease a large skillet with oil, heating til hot. Pour in one tablespoon of batter for each pancake. Cook over medium-high heat until edges brown (30-45 seconds). Keep pancakes warm on a plate in oven.

Huevos Rancheros Salsa

Ingredients:

6 large ripe tomatoes (or 1 large can peeled)
1 green bell pepper
2 yellow onions
2 Tbsps. chopped cilantro
1 small can of diced jalapeño peppers
Mexican hot sauce of your choice
2 Tbsps. olive oil

Method:

Cut the tomatoes and onions in half, slice and put in sauce pan with oil. Cut the bell pepper into small lengths and add to sauce pan. Simmer over low heat. Add jalapeños and hot sauce to taste. When cooked and ready to serve, add chopped cilantro.

Huevos Rancheros

Ingredients:

whole wheat tortillas
2 eggs (per serving)
grated cheddar cheese
salsa (recipe above)
cilantro
avacado and fruit slices

Method:

Warm a tortilla (whole wheat) and place on plate. Then fry two eggs and put them on top of the tortilla. Sprinkle with grated cheese and cover with salsa. Add a few sprigs of cilantro. Serve with black bean pancakes, slices of avocado and fresh fruit.

ERNESTO SANCHEZ

Performer Ernesto Sanchez is continually surprised and elated by the twists and turns of his career as a performing artist. He often refers to events in his life and on stage as being "magic". And anyone who has seen him perform with masks, knows the power of his mastery of illusion.

Over the last four years, he has taken his performances to Mexico each year, to Guatemala twice and also Nicaragua, on government-sponsored tours, giving workshops and performances. This year he has been offered a two-month residency sponsored by the prestigious Bellas Artas at San Angel in Mexico City.

Last year he gave an East-West mask-making workshop in Bali, the first time a workshop like that has taken place in that country. This year, as a result of the mask-making workshop, he's been commissioned by Festival 2000 in San Francisco to create a mask dance on Bali, going there to create the dance for two months. "It'll be a one-man solo show about illusion," said Sanchez, "and it'll be about how man and cultures are often blinded by beauty."

What does he mean by magic? "When I tell this story, people say 'Oh, that stuff only happens to you, Ernesto,' " he began. "But I was coming home from a short tour on Maui, and it was about 9 a.m. in Tam Junction. I was hitch-hiking a ride home. I waited. And I waited. It was 10, 10:30, 11. Finally a BMW with two women went by. I hardly bothered to stick out my thumb. The car went by, then braked, then pulled over way down the road. The woman in the

car was a friend I hadn't seen in seven years, and at that very moment, just as she turned the corner, she had been telling her friend about me, and there I was. She was so flabbergasted, it took her a while to back up and pick me up."

But as magical as all this may be, he also knows the creative process well. "Artists live in chaos. Sometimes there's a payoff, sometimes not," he said. "Things can dry up or flourish. I don't know why. I'm just glad it's happening. I've been performing and working in the theatre for 19 years, but it's only in the last five that I've gotten my priorities clear. Having clear goals and sticking with them has made the difference."

"On the tours to Mexico I discovered a Latin quality to my work that I hadn't been aware of. It was a taste of something I wanted to pursue. My own heritage is Mexican; my father was born in Mexico. When they called me looking for a 'Spanish-speaking mime,' I accepted, even though I spoke very little Spanish. I didn't realize how funny that was for a long time. That tour developed into the performance 'Spanish Speaking Mime.'

"For years I tried to figure out what to call my work. People in this country automatically think a mime is a pantomime in white face doing illusion work. The word's taken a bum rap. I've even called myself a 'silent comedian' to get away from the stigma of the word 'mime.' Then someone called me a 'Mexican mime.' I thought, 'Maybe that's what it is.'"

Here is a hearty meal from a 'Mexican mime:'

Chorizo and Eggs

Ingredients:

1/2 chopped onion
oil for frying
1 link of John's handmade chorizo (you can buy at the Bolinas Market)
4-5 sliced mushrooms
3 eggs
diced cheese of your choice
avocado, sour cream and salsa for topping

Method:

Preheat a 12-inch skillet. Chop onion. Sauté onion in oil. Stir in one link of John's chorizo, breaking it up in pan. Chop up mushrooms. When almost cooked, throw in mushrooms. Crack in eggs. Don't break the yolks. Let the eggs fry until the whites get white. Then throw in some diced cheese and scramble up the eggs. Serve with avocado, sour cream and salsa.

SWEET THINGS

JESSE SCHWARTZ

A few turns out of Bolinas is the road to Paradise Valley, a picturesque and appropriately named place, with a few houses on a dirt road which bends around organically farmed land. On one brilliant fall day I met with Jesse Schwartz, the man who has quietly created the Living Tree Center, an apple orchard and nursery of 100 varieties of heritage apple trees on 3/4 acre of land next to Pine Gulch Creek.

Those of us who were raised on a "supermarket apple" of red or gold delicious should prepare for a taste-bud explosion. There are, among hundreds of varieties of apples in the world, apples that taste like bananas, cinnamon, nutmeg, allspice and sassafrass. There are apples that grow to eight inches in diameter; you need only one for a whole pie.

There's an apple from Russia, which is porcelain white outside, and an apple from Alaska that is snow white inside. There are pink apples, and apples from days of the Court of Louis XIV, the "Caville Blanc d'Hiver," containing more vitamin C than an orange.

Living Tree Center was conceived with deep concern for the vanishing rain forests and native forests of North America. A group of four people in 1980 formed the small business with lofty goals: "To restore the original and native forests of North America." Noted Schwartz:

"In 1620, some 1.08 billion acres was covered with native forest. Now only five percent remains. We have committed a sacrilege for which we can atone by returning trees to the land."

As we walked the boundaries of the nursery, Schwartz, like the proud father of a large family, recounted the characteristics of each apple tree and where each was found. "This was found near an abandoned gold mine in the Sierra country, an excellent keeper.... This one dates back to the Middle Ages in England, this one was found in an abandoned orchard in the Olema Valley... and this one we named Harold's Large Apple, because a fellow named Harold guided us to it. It has a nutty flavor and is aromatic and will fill a room with perfume."

The days of huge old apple trees are waning, however, for most apple trees sold today are created by grafting cuttings to a "semi-dwarfing root stock," which means trees only grow to 12 feet. "No one can deal with huge trees and 20-foot ladders," explained Schwartz, who didn't seem to harbor any nostalgia. "The apple is more adaptable than any other fruit," he continued. "There are varieties that grow in Alaska and some 'low chill' varieties which can set fruit in Southern California."

Here are two recipes from Jesse Schwartz and his partner John Kozak.

John Kozak's Famous Apple Sauce

Ingredients:

12 lbs. assorted apples
4 quince
1 tsp. cinnamon
1 tsp. nutmeg
1/2 tsp. allspice
1/2 tsp. mace
1/2 tsp. cloves
1/2 tsp. ginger
 1/2 tsp. coriander

Method:

Scrub outer surface of quince to remove fuzz. Leave peels on both apples and quince. Core both. Cut away damaged or bruised spots. Finely grate 4 quince, leaving peel on. Grate a few of the apples. Put in a heavy 12-quart pot and cook over low flame. This will form a soft mush to start cooking applesauce. Don't add water. Prepare rest of apples by slicing thin (1/16") slices. Cook on low flame. Stir every 5-10 minutes. Add all 7 spices after entire mixture is mushy. Total time: 1-1/2 hours on low flame, using heavy waterless cookware or cast iron pot. No sugar, no honey. Kids never ask for sweetening, just more. Makes 7 quarts.

Indian & Apple Pudding

Ingredients:

6 cups milk
1/2 cup yellow cornmeal (Indian meal)
2/3 cup molasses
2 Tbsp. butter
1 tsp salt
1/2 tsp. ground ginger
1/4 tsp. grated nutmeg
3 apples, peeled, cored and sliced thin
light cream (optional)

Method:

Preheat oven to 275 degrees. Scald 4 cups of the milk in the top of a double boiler over direct heat, then place over boiling water.

Gradually add corn meal to the hot milk and cook, stirring constantly, until mixture is thick.

Add molasses, butter salt, ginger, and nutmeg.

Remove from heat and stir in remaining 2 cups of cold milk. Grease a 3-quart baking dish and put in a layer of the cornmeal mixture. Spread apple slices over that, then put in more cornmeal mixture and apples, alternating until you have 2 or 3 complete layers. Bake 3 hours in a preheated oven. Slice pudding, put into serving dishes while hot, and top each portion of pudding with light cream, if desired. Serves 12.

SALLY STEARNS

The passion for horses struck early for Sally Stearns of Bolinas. It started "with collections of plastic horse statues, and endless galloping around with a rope in hands for reins," recalled Stearns with a smile. "I finally convinced my parents to buy me a 28-year-old pony named Puddle Jumper for $100."

According to Stearns's theory, this "horse wack-o-ness" hits one woman in every generation, since her two brothers and sister seem to be unafflicted. She took out a photo of a young woman astride a large mare. "Aunt Evelyn was the last one. Her family owned a lumber business in Idaho."

Five years ago, Stearns realized what must be every 10-year-old girl's dream — to be the owner of a horse ranch. On this spring morning, Bolinas's Vanishing Point Ranch made an awfully pretty picture: a red and white rambling old farm house and matching new barn with eight stalls, tack and feed room, opening onto a spacious skylit breezeway. Outside in various paddocks, 15 horses grazed lazily on several acres of grass.

Stearns learned horsemanship through membership in local/national Pony Clubs, and as a girl began competing in what's called "Three-day eventing competitions," consisting of same horse/same rider events in dressage, cross-country and stadium jumping. "When I was 21, Maggie and I were Western State champions." She pointed to a horse lying prone in the grassy far pasture. "She's 28 now, old girl."

"Pony Club is a great way for kids to learn horsemanship. They learn it all: horse care, training, and showing, and it isn't expensive. Pony Club doesn't mean they ride ponies. The term originated in England and refers to any kid's mount. They can be members until they are 21."

Stearns co-founded the Marin Pony Club 12 years ago in Nicasio. Now she trains Pony Clubbers and adult horse-and-rider teams (ages five to 60) in showmanship. "I teach the first two levels of dressage, which is like training a horse to dance. They are stretched, warmed up and taken to their full athletic abilities ...With the little kids, I give a vaulting class. The horse moves on a lead in a circle and kids learn to get on and off while the horse is moving — no reins or stirrups. They really love it. Sometimes adult riders come to get help training for shows ... We had one little girl who went to the top in the national ratings."

But, no, she doesn't rent horses. "That's the question people ask me the most," said Stearns. You need to bring your own. She does board horses, when there's room, but right now she's got 15 horses besides her own and she's full up.

Here is a recipe from Sally Stearns's grandmother, May Stearns, enjoyed, no doubt, by lumberjacks of the past, somewhere up in Idaho.

Chocolate Sundae Pie

Ingredients:

1 baked pie crust
1-1/2 cups milk
3/4 cup sugar
3 egg yolks
1 envelope gelatin
3 egg whites
1 tsp. vanilla
whipped cream
slivered bittersweet chocolate

Method:

In a double boiler heat milk and 1/2 cup sugar until warm. Add beaten egg yolks. Dissolve gelatin in 1/4 cup cold water. When first mixture coats a spoon, add gelatin. Pour into a bowl to cool. Beat egg whites until stiff. Add 1/4 cup sugar and fold into custard. Flavor with vanilla. Pour into pie crust. Top with whipped cream and chocolate. Cool until served.

MARY BETH BRAUN

When documentary filmmakers Mary Beth Braun and Jim Heddle first moved to Bolinas, news of their work in Palau, a small island republic and former US territory in Micronesia, quickly spread through town. Palauans were the first nation to draw up a constitution declaring their territory a nuclear-free zone.

And Braun and Heddle have made it their business to let the world know, in the form of an award-winning documentary film narrated by Joanne Woodward (and an ongoing supply of footage to UN hearings), how our government reacts to such independent policy-making, given its military interest in the Pacific.

Mary Beth is a small, vibrant woman with electric blue eyes. Her looks belie her years, and her sense of purpose is as fierce as it is warm. "Nuclear annihilation is antithetical to the human spirit," she said, "and everyone ... has a right to say 'no' to nuclear substances on their land."

Fourteen years ago, Mary Beth Braun was an executive receptionist at Dow Chemical in Midland, Michigan. "It was a slow awakening," she explained. "I began to realize what was happening to the planet and talked to people about it. I was active in the community, I had even been a precinct delegate ... for the Republican party!

"I had it made: a gorgeous house on 16 acres, married, with two daughters. We skied and played tennis with the boss. We were in the upper one percent of earners of the world.

"But with understanding comes responsibility. I thought, 'The planet needs such help. Why would a billion years of creation stop with us?' So I completely let go. I took $200 and left for Washington, D.C. I felt like I was jumping off a cliff, but I knew somehow it would work out. My family thought I had gone crazy. My mother thought I'd gone into a cult and become a Communist.

"In Washington, I met Jim (Heddle), a professor of psychotherapy and filmmaker. When I visited Jim I learned of the Palau project, their struggle to maintain their right to be nuclear-free, and I decided to commit myself to that work. At first I did anything that needed to be done — fundraising, phone calls, networking. I was so thirsty for meaningful work, after knowing people whose only thought was what they would buy next."

Since the release of the film, Mary Beth has become a producer/director in her own right, as well as co-director (with Heddle) of their information-production service. Their service offers video, film and radio consultation, investigative reporting, and supplies footage for hearings in Washington, D.C and around the globe. The film was also a catalyst for the development of an international organization, co-directed by Braun and Heddle, called "The Nuclear Sovereignty Project."

"We try to establish irrefutable documentation to combat disinformation on issues. The US is still vulnerable to public pressure. We hope to reinspire the people in these nations, who lose faith that their way of living is worth fighting for."

This recipe was created by Jim Heddle and is recommended only for serious garlic lovers of West Marin.

Fresh Banana Coconut Pie

Ingredients:

Pie Crust:
Any mixture of raw nuts will do, such as walnuts or almonds. Makes a 9" pie crust.
3/4 -1 cup ground nuts
        (in blender or food processor)
3/4 cup chopped figs
1/2 tsp. cinnamon

Filling:
6 medium bananas, mashed by hand
1 cup fresh grated coconut
1 splash of vanilla
sliced strawberries, kiwi, bananas and other fruits
edible flowers such as nasturtiums, sweet borage and pansies

Method:

Pie crust:
   Mix together nuts and figs by hand and pat into a pie plate.

Filling:
   Mash bananas by hand, and add coconut and vanilla. Pour into pie crust. Decorate the top with colorful sliced fruit and fresh flowers. Make it gorgeous. Chill the pie for at least one hour before serving.

LINDA SAMUELS

Artist and curator Linda Samuels of Bolinas is busy with two galleries now; she was selected as the curator of exhibitions and programs for Falkirk Cultural Center in San Rafael in addition to her guest curatorship of the Bolinas Museum.

"I'm interested in accessible art," she said. "Art which people don't have to ask, 'What is this?' And I'm interested in how art influences people's lives. The older I get, the more I realize things begin where you live...Your life starts at your front door ... so I figure out ways to work art back into our lives."

It's not surprising, then, that her first show at Falkirk was called "The Home Show," a playful selection of 12 artists' works relating to objects found in the home. There were refrigerators and radios that lit up, or opened up, with beautifully rendered scenes inside.

Falkirk Center is a large Victorian home on 11 acres— a beautiful space, but not what you think of as a gallery. It has fireplaces, bedrooms and staircases. Her plan is to create a forum for artists in the form of a monthly "slide night" — an opportunity for artists to see what's being done elsewhere, and a free noon concert on the grounds for shoppers to gather and eat lunch to music.

Meanwhile, Samuels volunteers two days a week for her pet project as guest curator of the non-profit Bolinas Museum. "We're trying to make it a more community-based project, by exhibiting not only historical artifacts, but what local artists are doing now," Samuels said. "I've been choosing artwork for the Living Artists Project. We have over 80 working artists. For a village our size that's an amazing statistic."

Samuels's art training began on the East Coast, when, after entering Brown University bound for a career as a writer, she found that the "folks in the art department looked more like I did." She switched to an art major, working in sculpture. Continuing on, she received a Master of Fine Arts from Cranbrook Academy of Art in Detroit in print making and sculpture.

"In the 60s, after you got your MFA, you taught college. I married, moved to Texas and taught art at Southern Methodist University. At that time, there was only one gallery in Dallas, and in an attempt to find a place to show my work, I joined with seven other women to form a Woman's Cooperative Gallery. I directed it for seven years. We expanded three times. I was very proud of that gallery. We gave a lot of better known Texas artists their first shows. I was invited to curate their last show."

Here's a recipe from Linda Samuels's home kitchen.

Fruit Betty Pie

Ingredients:

1 pie shell
7-8 mangoes (or nectarines, peaches or berries)
1 cup brown sugar
1 cup flour
1/2 cup butter
3/4 cup chopped pecans

Method:

Cut and skin 7-8 mangoes (nectarines, peaches, berries will do). Fill the pie shell with fruit. Sprinkle 1/2 cup of brown sugar on fruit. In another bowl put: 1 cup flour, 1/2 cup butter, mix it up, until it looks like cornmeal. Add 1/2 cup brown sugar, chopped pecans. Knead this mixture and pat it out and lay on top of fruit. Bake 1 hour in a 350-degree oven.

ANNIE CROTTS

Postmaster Annie Crotts is a well-known and loved figure in Bolinas. She's worked at the post office since 1960, but it was only five or six years ago that she finally accepted the postmastership. Crotts is also the high soprano soloist who sings the Star Spangled Banner each year to kick off Bolinas's annual Fourth of July parade. She's been hitting that high "C" since 1938.

Annie May (Wagner) first came to Bolinas at the age of two, with her family from Marion, Massachusetts. Her father, Walter, was appointed chief rigger at the RCA station, a sending station for overseas communications on the windy bluff by the Commonweal buildings on Mesa Road. That was in February, 1925.

"We had a little wooden cottage by the cliffs, out there," Annie said slowly, as if the memory was coming back, bit by bit. "In the spring, the whole point was full of wild strawberries — enough to make a batch of pies. There was more bluff there then, and a grove of pine trees and a fence. The road past the powerhouses went down to the beach. I remember getting wood on the beach — and clamming, musseling, and fishing for bass and eel.

"There were these soft-shelled clams, we'd find embedded in the shale. You'd rake up the rocks, and tap them. They'd fall apart, and a small oval-shaped clam would be there. I don't know what kind they were, but there were lots of them."

Every Saturday, Annie's father would work for a half day, then come home, eat lunch and take the whole family "over the hill" to San Rafael in the family car. They shopped, ate dinner and often saw a show. "But few folks in San Rafael had ever heard of Bolinas," said Annie.

Piano lessons for Annie began at the age of nine, from Maxine Pepper until she decided she wanted to sing. "At the time, we had a chorus at the school, and I found I had a high voice. So Mrs. Pepper said she'd give me singing lessons instead."

"Mrs. Pepper was leading the Fourth of July singing at the time I was in high school .... Somehow I got to sing the Star Spangled Banner. I can remember standing on those steps of the building that used to be the Coast Guard building [now the Marine Biology Station]. We've always stood on those same steps to start off the parade. In those days it was just a little parade. There was a lot more beach then and more wood to make fires. The big event was the great big bonfire on the beach at night and of course fireworks. The Pomeroy family built a trench and set off great splashing sprays of fireworks. We were very fortunate to have a display so fine and fancy."

Annie opened a bound, weathered cookbook of her mother Alice's which contained recipes in fountain pen script from 1920. This recipe was one of those inside. It cooks to a cake-custard consistency when done correctly.

Lemon Sponge Pie

Ingredients:

1 c. sugar
2 Tbsp. butter
2 egg yolks
juice and rind of 1 lemon
3 Tbsp. flour
1 cup milk
2 egg whites
1 pie crust

Method:

Beat together sugar, butter and egg yolks. Add juice and rind of lemon, sprinkle in flour. Mix altogether, adding 1 cup milk. Beat 2 egg whites until stiff. Fold them into the mixture. Pour entire mixture into a pie crust. Bake for 45 minutes in a "slow oven" which Annie and I guess to be approximately 325 degrees.

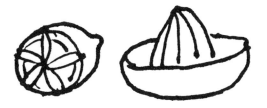

JEREMIAH ABRAMS

Inverness therapist and author Jeremiah Abrams' new book, *Reclaiming the Inner Child*, is the first of three which Abrams contracted to write for publication by Jeremy Tarcher Inc., the same folks who published *Women Who Love Too Much*, and *Chop Wood, Carry Water*.

It's an anthology of 37 essays by noted psychologists, philosophers and scholars, such as Joseph Campbell, Eric Ericson and Alice Miner, relating to the theme of the "inner child."

The publication of the book, Abrams says, represents an emergence of his own, "a move out of the consulting room and into life."

"Writing the book has been the least of it," he said. "I wrote perhaps on- sixth of the book. I collected everything I could find relevant to the theme. The 'inner child' has seen a lot of use in this culture. It is an important symbol for recovery. And, as Jung said, "For those who have a symbol it is easier to change'."

"The timing of this book is good," explained Abrams. "In the 1970s, drugs and addiction were not big issues. Today the inner child has a resonance with many, especially those trying to overcome compulsive behavior. Anyone can go in and read an entry of this book and walk away with something useful and pertinent for his/her life."

Abrams' 20-year career as a therapist began with studying alternative therapies at Cambridge in the late 60s. Remember encounter groups, "plunges" and "sensitivity training?" While doing graduate work at Boston University, he co-founded a family therapy training institute. In the early 1970s he met a Jungian analyst and "aggressively" began training in analysis and dreamwork.

In 1979, Abrams and his wife came to Inverness, where together they have founded the Mount Vision Institute in Sausalito and Inverness.

"My approach is that we are all walking wounded, in some sense," explained Abrams with a thoughtful pause as he searched for the most precise possible wording, "and our lives are a process of integration and individuation — finding your purpose in life. The word psychotherapy means literally 'care of the soul' — your inner reality."

A believer in the proverbial cup of tea with any conversation, Jeremiah Abrams served this almond biscotti, with hot apricot tea for dunking. It was delicious.

Jeremiah Abrams' Almond Biscotti

Ingredients:

1 cup sugar
1/2 cup unsalted butter
3 Tbsp. Brandy
1 Tbsp. vanilla
1 Tbsp. almond extract
1-1/2 tsp. baking powder
1 tsp. salt
1 cup toasted sliced almonds
3 eggs
2-1/2 to 3 cup flour

Method:

In your mixer, mix sugar, butter, brandy, vanilla and almond extracts, baking powder and salt together with about 2/3 of the nuts and the eggs. Put about 2 cups of flour in and mix. Take this very sticky result out and let sit on a large board with some of the remaining flour on it for a few minutes. Add rest of nuts and work the rest of the flour into the batter. Form in two French bread-looking loaves.

Bake on a sheet at 350 degrees for 1/2 hour. Remove and cool. Slice loaf into diagonal slices, 1/2 inch thick. Return to oven on sheet and bake for 25 minutes at 350 degrees, turning once. Take care here not to burn. Remove and cool. If desired, dip on side in melted chocolate and allow to harden.

HENRY IASIELLO

In the kitchen something heavenly was baking and the espresso maker brewing. Henry Iasiello and his six-year-old son Kelson had the house to themselves; wife and daughter were away for the weekend. So far, it didn't look half bad.

"This is our project for the day," said Henry, opening up the oven to check on a blackberry pie which bubbled under a criss-cross pattern of a browning crust. "We do it all together: discovering life in the berry patch, the spiders and the bees, to eating the pie. It's a big thing with me. I believe kids need to spend real time with adults doing real things."

Henry and Jane made a mutual decision before having kids. They decided to make enough money so that they didn't have to work full time when the kids were growing up. When they had enough they'd stop. Many are not so fortunate, and bills have a way of exceeding expectations, but so far, they've stuck to their plan.

"Kids are the ones who pay for our lifestyles," said Iasiello. "They don't relate well to the commuter lifestyle, where there is a great separation between the child's world and the adult world. I decided to spend some time in the child's world. Spending time with your kids slows your life down a lot. But this is my priority. I say, 'I don't have time to work now. My kid needs me.'

"In a boys' group, position in the group is their first concern. They'll fight to be the leader. Boys learn to form their identities in terms of separateness. If someone gets hurt, well tough, that's life ... But girls, I think because they often have a more accessible role model (Mom, all day), have a more refined sense of the web of interrelationship. Girls will often end the game before leaving someone out."

Iasiello has also observed the effect television has had on his children. "TV is like an oral tradition. If you listen to these kids talking to each other at school, it sounds like gibberish if you haven't seen the shows they watch.

"TV is also like food. You don't feed your kids something you wouldn't feed yourself. If there's a question about a show, they don't watch unless I'm there watching with them. Sometimes I tape things so we can stop and discuss things, like violence, or commercial 'jingles.'

"You can count on kids for tremendous amounts of love. They'll turn themselves into pretzels to please the adults they love. In a way, they are almost much too willing to sacrifice themselves for the people they love."

Father and Son Blackberry Pie

Ingredients:

Filling:
 1 cup sugar
 8 cups berries
 3 Tbsp. Minute tapioca

Crust:
 2 cups flour
3-5 Tbsp. sugar
2/3 cup margarine or shortening
1 tsp. salt

Method:

Filling:
 Be sure to delegate tasks: father can turn oven on, kid can set the temperature (450 degrees, then 350 degrees) Mix filling ingredients together, in a large bowl let sit while you make the crust.

Crust:
 In a large bowl, place shortening, sugar and salt. Break up the margarine into smaller pieces. Add flour gradually, mixing it into the margarine until it holds together in a ball. Roll it out on a floured surface. It'll make enough crust for top and bottom or generous lattice work. Father can roll out the crust, kid can cut lattices and pinch edges of pie crust around pie plate. Pour berry mixture into pie shell. Top with strips. Bake at 450 degrees for 10 minutes, 350 degrees for 45 minutes more.

MAYE ADAMS

Over a steamy cup of cinnamon-spiced tea, I spoke with Maye Adams at the kitchen counter of her Inverness home. To many children in West Marin, Maye Adams is the lady who greets them each day in a yellow school bus. At the moment, she was between morning and afternoon routes. She'd been up since 4 a.m.—a routine of 17 years now. "I look forward to the weekends when I can sleep in until 6 a.m," she joked.

Her Midwestern background is ever-present in her unpretentious warmth. She is not inclined to boast her considerable accomplishments: prize-winning pie maker, professional tailor, gardener and mother of four.

Born and raised in Oklahoma, for Adams the home-making arts are second nature. "I learned these things at my mother's knee ... quilting, sewing, knitting, crocheting, cooking ... I learned to cook for our family [of seven] early on," she said.

Hard times in Oklahoma during World War II forced her mother to relocate the family to California. Maye recalls the trip as a 16-year - old: "I hated California. We drove out in a hot car across the desert with five kids in the car. But the shipyards in Richmond and the Bay Area were booming because of the war effort. My mother and I both found work in restaurants."

"When I was 24, we came to West Marin to manage a small restaurant located where Chez Madeleine is now. Both my sister and I met the men we married at that restaurant. And we've been here ever since."

Adams's reputation as a baker of sumptuous pies and desserts probably began with her own family. "The Adams family has an incredible sweet tooth," she said. But not all of her baking stories are success stories.

Adams described her first entry in the Western Weekend pie contest. "A few years ago I entered the pie contest ... I made two lemon pies and started down the hill here from the house, with my pies on the seat, trying to go real slow. A car came up the hill fast, and I had to put on the brakes, and ... Pssshoot! Both pies slid onto the floor. So I just turned around and came home. It was too late to bake anything else. Oh, I was so *angry.*"

She made up for it: she's been the undefeated blue ribbon pie maker of Point Reyes Station's Western Weekend every year since. In fact, each year a pie is auctioned to benefit various causes. One went for $30.

Here is Maye Adams's generously given, prize-winning apple pie recipe. She says it makes a big, 12-inch pie.

Maye Adams's Blue-Ribbon Apple Pie

Ingredients:

No fail pie crust:
2 cups flour
1 cup shortening (Crisco)
1 tsp. salt
1/4 cup flat 7-up or Ginger Ale

Filling:
6-8 good-sized apples
1 cup crushed pineapple
2 heaping Tbsps. flour
1/4 tsp. cinnamon
1/4 tsp. nutmeg
3/4 cup sugar
1-2 Tbsp. butter
lemon juice of 1/2 lemon

Method:

Makes one large, 12-inch pie

No fail pie crust:
Use a large, 12-inch pie plate. Mix the salt and flour and then cut in the shortening. Add the 7-up, sprinkling a little at a time and roll out dough on a floured surface. Makes a top and bottom crust.

Filling:
Mix flour, sugar, and spices. Core, peel and slice apples, and layer apples, then pineapple, then sprinkle with spice mixture. Before the top crust, put 4 pats of butter on apples and 1 table-spoon lemon juice. Make holes in top crust for steam. Bake at 425 degrees for 10-15 minutes, then turn down to 350 degrees and bake for 45 minutes or until apples are done.

PHIL GINOLFI

Chef extraordinaire of Bolinas, many have said, Phil Ginolfi learned to cook at the knees of Hungarian and Sicilian grandmothers. His passion for cooking is such that he is known to wake up, head straight for the kitchen, and begin making Hungarian dumplings at 8 a.m.

His story begins outside New York City where he grew up. "Christmastime meant good food," he began, "and my Hungarian grandmother lived above the family butcher shop. When I was five, I cranked the grinder for her, for bread crumbs, ground meat — she used it for everything. Since my uncles were hunters, we'd often have pheasant, duck and venison on Christmas. I used to pluck the birds — hey, it's not easy... I'd sit with a bucket of water, because you have to dip them so the down doesn't get all over you."

"On Christmas Eve, we'd go to her apartment, to a giant oak table stretched to fit 15. She'd have cooked for days: poppyseed cakes, cookies, walnut-filled flaky strudels, and a roast beef dinner with all the trimmings."

On Christmas Day, it was his Sicilian grandmama's turn to impress. "We literally drooled, going up the stairs to her apartment. She was an artist. She'd make stuffed, deboned chickens and homemade ravioli the size of your fist, artichoke heart salads, oh, and all kinds of Italian pastries — ricotta cheese pies, anisette cookies, and tiny ones covered with honey and sprinkles... I still stand in awe of pastry chefs. That's an exact science. I'm not that exacting a cook, I like to experiment and estimate, but you can't do that with pastries..."

"I learned most of my hands-on cooking from friends (chili rellenos, vegetarian dishes) or travels. In Japan, I learned how to make breakfast (roasted eggplant, miso and vegetables) on top of a mulberry leaf. I'd go to the markets and point to a strange fish or one of the many mushroom varieties and ask 'How you cook?' But I learned sushi from watching good sushi chefs right here in California.

"The other thing I love to do is hunt for wild herbs and mushrooms. I've studied ethnobotany and mycology for 15 years... but I'm very cautious with mushrooms. Except for the foolproof four, I take the advice of experts: admire them and leave them alone."

Here is a traditional, but simple, recipe for Christmas Eve, or any eve, for that matter.

Italian Frangelico Pie

Ingredients:

Pie Crust:
1-1/2 packages Pepperidge Farm
 Hazelnut cookies
1/2 stick soft, sweet butter

Filling:
2 packages (15 oz.) Ricotta cheese
16 oz. white chocolate chips (dark will do nicely,
but changes the color)
4 oz. Frangelico liqueur (hazelnut flavored)

Method:

Pie Crust:
 Crush cookies in a blender or by hand. Mix in
butter with hands, until the mixture is uniform in
texture. Press into 12" pie plate with spoon.

Filling:
 Melt white chocolate chips in double boiler.
Put ricotta cheese and liqueur in blender. Blend,
adding melted chocolate to the cheese mixture as
it is blending. Pour into pie shell. Chill. Top with
chopped nuts and shaved chocolate curls.

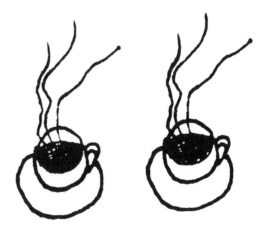

DAVE SOBEL

Under his white baker's apron, Dave Sobel wore, among other things, a tie-dyed T-shirt, tie-dyed socks and Birkenstock sandals. It's a political statement, as are many of the policies and practices of the Bolinas Bay Bakery, which Dave owns in downtown Bolinas.

"I enjoy dressing this way," he said with a grin. "People smile when they look at me. In this business you're selling emotional nourishment as much as baked goods." The bakery has become Dave's expression of social consciousness in many ways.

"We've been setting a precedent," he explained, "for instance by going to organic flour. We're the first bakery in Marin to use only organic flour. I think it makes a nuttier flavor. It costs 15 more cents a pound, but it supports sustainable agriculture. We use paper cups rather than styrofoam. We use all butter, no margarine, and oat bran."

The list of recipients of Bolinas Bay Bakery donations would fill a small phone directory. To name a few, the bakery has supported the Rainforest Action Network, Greenpeace, Earth First, SEVA Foundation,

Bread and Roses, the Point Reyes Bird Observatory, M.O.W., local school groups, and individual birthday parties. "I just donated until I was accepted by the town. How do you know when you're accepted? I guess when you feel accepted."

Before coming to Bolinas, Dave worked for anti-nuclear groups at Vandenburg and Diablo Canyon. At Diablo he ran the "hippie kitchen" for the demonstrators, feeding 2,500 people with no refrigeration and constant supervision by health inspectors.

He's worked as an Emergency Medical Technician for United Ambulance, for the Humane Society doing rescue work, and coordinated Red Cross mass feeding efforts during the '83 and '86 floods. As he sums himself up, "Logistics are my forté."

Cooking is also one of Dave's fortés. Dave studied at the Cordon Bleu School in London.

His talents will come in handy, since Sobel's next project is to move the Bolinas Bay Bakery to its new site across the street from the little house where it is now located. The new location will offer seating, and cafe-style breakfast and lunch fare.

Here is a recipe from Dave Sobel's kitchen.

Fresh Raspberry Baked Alaska

Ingredients:

2 baskets fresh raspberries
1 single layer cake (vanilla)
2 pints Ben & Jerry's vanilla ice cream
Bacardi 151 Rum
6 egg whites
 pinch of cream of tartar
1 cup sugar

Method:

On a single cake layer, place the two baskets of fresh raspberries. Allow ice cream to soften, and when it's workable, mound the ice cream on top of the raspberries and cake layer. Place in freezer. Whip egg whites, adding the cream of tartar; as they stiffen, add the sugar. Spread egg white over ice cream cake. Take 1/2 egg shell, place it on top of the cake face up, as a tiny cup for the rum, later. Put in 450 degree oven until golden brown (3-6 minutes). Dim the lights. Pour rum into egg shell, and light it as you carry out the cake to serve.

KATHY LOVE

The unmistakable aroma of fresh-baked chocolate chip cookies lured all of the kids into the kitchen from their games in the yard. No doubt about it, Kathy Love of Point Reyes Station knows how to make a Sunday afternoon taste nearly perfect.

"I love to bake things," said Love, as she passed out the chewy, hot morsels to each pair of reaching hands. "Especially desserts. They're my specialty... the decadent ones. I don't fudge on the rich stuff, which of course is all very fattening."

How does she stay so slim with such a sweet tooth? "It's an optical illusion," she kidded. "I wear baggy clothes." The truth is, she's unusually active and energetic. She is a nurse on Marin General's orthopedic/neurological floor three days a week. She's secretary and parent representative for the School Council. She spends one day a week in a classroom at the school, she's mother of two sons: and is "the major support system for a husband who coaches Little League in the spring and soccer in the fall."

It seems it's always been this way for Love, who was raised in southern California with five brothers and a mother who welcomed the bustle of children and friends in the house. "My mother baked a lot, so I picked it up. It smelled so good to have something baking. And it always tastes so much better when you make it from scratch."

"I grew up in a neighborhood where every family for blocks around had between five and nine kids. You never knew how many would sit down for dinner at night," she recalled.

After she's finished with work and has taken care of her family, she still finds time for herself. "That's when I pick up my girl friend and go to the Estero Trail for a walk or a bike ride. There are so many secluded and beautiful places you can go out here."

Love has lived in West Marin for 13 years and feels strongly that this is a rare and wonderful community to live in. "I love living out here. I like having five acres, having my kids run outside in fresh air... I wouldn't give it up. I'm really proud of the people, the school and the community here."

Here's one of Kathy Love's popular desserts. She says it's good with other fruits, if raspberries are not in season.

Fresh Raspberry Tart with Lemon Cream

Ingredients:

Shortbread pastry:
1/2 cup sugar
3/4 cup butter or margarine.
1 large egg yolk
2 cups unsifted cake flour

Filling:
2 large egg yolks
6 Tbsp. sugar
2 Tbsp. lemon juice
1/4 cup (1/8 lb.) unsalted butter
1 baked pastry shell (recipe follows)
1-1/2 to 2 cups raspberries, rinsed (or fruit in season)

Method:

Shortbread pastry:
   With an electric mixer, cream together sugar and butter. Thoroughly mix in egg yolk, then cake flour. Spread in springform pan and bake for about 20 minutes in 400-degree oven until light brown.

Filling:
   In a 3- to 4-cup saucepan, with a rubber spatula, stir yolks, sugar, lemon juice and butter over medium-low heat until butter melts and mixture is thick, about 12 minutes. Remove from heat. Let cool. Spread lemon cream in pastry. Arrange berries neatly over cream.

ELLY SIMMONS

Artist Elly Simmons's phone rang about every 10 minutes. Sometimes she'd converse in Spanish, sometimes in English, always with an apology for being busy and a promise to call back. A glance around the interior of her home reveals colorful political posters and paintings, a desk overflowing with paperwork, and a refrigerator door completely covered with notes and invitations.

A painter and activist, living in Lagunitas, Elly has combined her interest in politics with her talent as an artist so successfully that even she seems surprised by her recent popularity; she's done several other interviews for publication recently.

She's active with Marin Center for Peace and Justice, does posters for the Christic Institute, and is a panel member of the Art and Issues series sponsored by the Bolinas Museum and Falkirk Cultural Center (where she recently showed her work in a show entitled "Our Town: Art and Politics"). She did the Canto American album cover, supports Amnesty International, is working on a collaborative project with weavers for the rainforest, illustrated an El Salvadoran children's story. And we've hardly begun.

She was invited to be part of the San Francisco-Leningrad Ecological Arts Collaboration Project, an exchange whereby ecologists and artists met to study Bay Area environmental problems and do collaborative artwork around the environmental theme. In this case, both Leningrad and San Francisco had water problems which were studied by the group, in each location.

"The Russian people love the arts and discuss them avidly," she said. "Activists there [in Leningrad] felt that artists are the link, and found it urgent that artists speak out on environmental issues." For five weeks, Leningrad artists toured San Francisco with American artists.

"I focus on human rights issues. It's easy to love a whale or a rainforest, because it doesn't have a different ideological base. Lots of people will work on saving the rainforest, so I tend to focus on the people of an area.

"People tend to think of those involved in progressive politics as too serious and negative," she continued. "But I find just the opposite is true. Work that is anti-war or anti-racist is life-affirming, positive aspect of humanity. I end up having a lot of fun, working and dancing with people who have a real love of life."

Elly encourages those inclined to make a one-of-a-kind customized cheesecake for a friend. Using little symbols, (tzatzkehs, in Yiddish) like toy boats, turtles, an old superman statue, flowers and fruits for color, she usually follows a theme inspired by the person's interests and goes hog wild from there.

But the base of her fabulous cakes is the trusty old New York cheesecake, from her grandmother who lived on the lower east side.

Grandmother's New York-Style Cheesecake

Ingredients:

Crumb crust:
1 tsp. sugar
4-5 Tbsp. melted butter
1-1/2 cup graham cracker crumbs

Filling:
1 lb. cream cheese
4 eggs
1/3-1/2 cup sugar
2 Tbsp. lemon juice
3/4 tsp. vanilla extract
3/4 tsp. almond extract
pinch salt

Topping:
1 pt. sour cream
3/4 tsp. vanilla
1/3 cup sugar
1 Tbsp. lemon juice

Method:

Crumb crust:
 Mix in a bowl. Spread evenly in bottom of pie pan. Press firmly against sides and bottom.

Filling:
 Blend well, mixing with hands. Honest. Cream it with your hands. Pour into crumb crust. Bake at 350 degrees for 25 minutes Cool on rack 1 hour.

Topping:
 Blend together sour cream, vanilla, sugar and lemon juice. Pour on top of filling. Bake for 5-10 minutes. Cool. Refrigerate. Decorate with baubles, fruit and candies.

MATT PREBLUTAL

It was New Year's Day, 1981, when 15-year-veteran-baker Matt Preblutal woke up after a Grateful Dead concert and signed the papers for the new business known as the Knave of Hearts Bakery. Today, when he's not baking, his passion for the "Dead" has been replaced by the Giants and he says he and his wife buy season tickets and go to at least two games a week.

Prebluda's casual wit and off-handed manner beguile the daily rigors of owning a bakery. The job keeps either wife Robin or Matt working nearly 'round the clock. Robin works the midnight shift, making breads and pastries; then Matt takes over making cakes, desserts and brunch items, such as quiches and stuffed croissants. Their son, in school at Drake High, leaves between their shifts.

It was a rough start, with the floods of 1982 wiping out the business. "There was five feet of mud at the counter where you're sitting," said Prebluda. "In the early 1980s it was a hangout for carpenters who packed the place, drinking coffee until 10 a.m. Then in the mid 80s, most of them

had car payments, kids and mortgages, and little time for a coffee stop."

Then the tourist business picked up. "Since Point Reyes [National Seashore] has been discovered, business is excellent. Seventy-five percent of it is return customers from out of town."

Knave of Hearts wholesales baked goods to the Marin Farmer's Market, Petaluma Farmer's Market, Bolinas People's Store, the Point Reyes Seashore Lodge and many of the bed-and-breakfast lodges in the area.

Here is a lip-smacking recipe replete with Matt Prebluda's helpful tips. My confidential baking consultant tells me his pastry-making style is classically French; his delicacies some of the finest in the Bay Area.

Creme Patisserie

Ingredients:

Shortbread pastry:
1/2 lb. sweet butter (2 sticks)
2 egg yolks
1 tsp. baking powder
2 cup flour
splash cognac
1/2 cup sugar

Pastry Cream Filling:
2 vanilla beans
1 pint milk
3 egg yolks
2 eggs
3/8 cup cornstarch
3/4 cup sugar
1 pint heavy cream

Method:

Shortbread pastry:
Preheat oven to 400 degrees. Cream butter and sugar. Mix in the yolks. Add dry ingredients and cognac. Mix just until it combines to a solid dough, then stop. Press into a greased 8 "x 10" flan or quiche tin by hand. Tip: Place a greased cake pan on top while baking so it doesn't rise unevenly. Bake. Check after 15 minutes to see if it's brown but not overcooked. Never trust a recipe. Cool pastry. Go on to the filling.

Pastry Cream Filling:
Split vanilla beans down middle and scrape out insides into milk. It'll look like dirty milk. Boil milk and 1/2 sugar. In another bowl whisk egg yolks, whole eggs, other half of sugar, cornstarch and cognac. In one hand you're boiling milk, the other whisking egg mixture. With third hand, take a ladle of milk and pour into egg mixture while whipping. This warms the egg mixture so you don't get boiled eggs. Pour the egg mixture, while vigorously stirring, into the milk mixture. In less than 10 seconds you have custard. Take off the flame. Put in refrigerator.

In mixer, whip up heavy cream until stiff. Remove vanilla bean remnants from custard. (Tip: Wash and save vanilla bean. They're expensive, so reuse it by putting it in a jar of powdered sugar to flavor.) Now with your hands, do the dog paddle, and fold the whipped cream and custard together. (Tip: You were born with two perfect spatulas. Make sure they are clean.) With a pastry-tube star tip, pipe or spread mixture in scribbled loops over the pastry layer. Decorate with fresh fruit, like a mandala. To glaze, melt down some commercial apricot jelly and brush over the fruit topping. Matt makes a hot glaze by boiling apricot nectar and corn syrup together.

HAROLD BUCKLIN

The air smells better on the top of Inverness Ridge. I noticed the freshness immediately as I walked up the woodsy path to the home of Harold Bucklin, a renowned hiker in the area. I felt like I'd been transported to a high Sierra pine forest.

With the vigor and stamina of a man of far fewer years, Bucklin, now past the 80-year mark, attributes his health to his weekly hikes of seven to 10 miles and life in this clean air. He's been hiking since 1970, when he and his wife Winona came to Inverness to build their home.

The "Tuesday Irregulars," also known as "Walkers and Talkers" is the name of the informal group of about 20 hikers who join Bucklin on his day-long treks throughout the Point Reyes National Seashore every Tuesday. "We meet at about 9:30 a.m. at an agreed-upon place," said Bucklin. "Then we decide which trail we're going to do. People come from quite a ways. One comes from China Camp, another from Healdsburg. And these days the women outnumber the men."

We spread out a map of the area on the dining room table and Bucklin pointed out some of his hikes. "Most of these trails were old ranch roads. Here's a good one," he said, pointing to the Ridge Trail to Pablo Point. We spotted a dark-colored mountain lion this summer up there.

We were downwind of him, and we were able to watch him for quite a while until he heard us and bounded away. But it was a mountain lion, all right, with a long tail — not a bobcat. No, it was a mountain lion."

Bucklin's hiking days began when a friend was hired to look after the trails for the newly formed National Seashore. They hiked all 75 miles of trails. "Somewhere here is the Bucklin Trail," he said, adding modestly, "I guess they ran short of names about then." Sure enough, there was the Bucklin trail, south of Bear Valley.

The Bucklins together have put herculean work into their homestead on the ridge. Winona designed their home, which they also helped build. Harold built and installed one of the area's first solar hot water heaters on the roof during the "oil crisis" of the 1970s. The terraced gardens are irrigated by a swimming-pool-sized covered cistern. A log splitter sits amidst piles of freshly split wood, ready for winter.

As Harold and I bit into these crunchy, buttery squares, called "Hello Dollies," Winona admonished him, "Only one." They are not on his diet. She is understandably proud: "Thirty years ago I read about reducing cholesterol to prevent heart disease... I think he looks very fit for his age, don't you?"

Hello Dollies

Ingredients:

1/4 lb. butter or margarine
12 oz. real chocolate bits
1-1/2 cup Corn Flake crumbs
1-1/2 cup chopped walnuts
1/2 cup all-purpose flour
1 can evaporated sweetened milk

Method:

Mix together butter, crumbs and flour, pat evenly into a buttered 9" x 13 pan. Sprinkle on chocolate, then walnuts. Warm the milk in a saucepan and drizzle top. Sprinkle on sesame seeds. Bake at 350 degrees for 30 minutes. Pass under the broiler for a few seconds to toast sesame seeds. Cut in squares while warm. Makes 48 cookies, 1-1/2" square. The texture is improved by freezing.

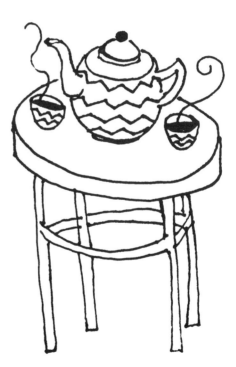

JOYCE GOLDFIELD

Co-founder of Halleck Creek Riding Club, Joyce Goldfield laughed when I asked about the cake she baked for a horse. She told the story of a horse named Freddy the Freeloader. The children who ride at Halleck Creek named him such because he wandered on to the ranch years ago.

When Freddy reached retirement age, the kids thought they should celebrate. They gussied him up in a shawl, braided his mane and tail, and served him a cake made with Bisquick and horse grain, complete with carrots for candles.

The occasion was made even more special by the enthusiasm of the children and adults Goldfield works with. They are physically handicapped, with disabilities ranging from cerebral palsy and muscular dystrophy to birth defects. What they all share is the challenge of overcoming their disabilities.

In 1977, Duane Irving of Nicasio, then horse trainer for rangers at the Point Reyes National Seashore, and Joyce Goldfield of Inverness Park recognized a need. "We took riding parties from various hospitals out into the parks, but there was always a child in a wheelchair who couldn't go.

We thought, if we could put them on our laps, they could see the parks, too," said Goldfield. And so Halleck Creek Riding Club was born.

Starting out with 12 kids and six horses, Joyce and Duane began a program for disabled children. Soon word spread, volunteers joined in, and children and adults from Marin, Sonoma, San Francisco and Contra Costa counties found their way to Halleck Creek.

Now the club includes 435 kids, 45 horses, and 150 volunteers. It is a bona fide 4-H Club program. Its activities include overnights on horseback, shooting the rapids on the Rogue River, snow trips to the Sierra, sailing, and, thanks to Goldfield's passion for baking, lots of good food.

"At age nine, my grandmother taught me 'everything you needed to know to catch a man,' which meant baking an apple pie, a gooey chocolate cake, roast beef and fried chicken," joked Goldfield. "Baking is still the thing I enjoy the most."

"Our kids are the greatest examples of courage, enthusiasm, joy and determination. They have every reason to be down on life, and they aren't at all," said Goldfield.

Joyce Goldfield's Toll House Cookies

Ingredients:

Makes 4-5 dozen.
2-1/4 cups flour
3/4 cups brown sugar (packed)
1 tsp. baking soda
1 tsp. vanilla
1 tsp. salt
2 eggs
1 cup butter
2 cups chocolate chips (12 oz.)
3/4 cup white sugar
1 cup coarsely chopped nuts

Method:

Preheat oven at 350 degrees. Combine butter, sugars, vanilla, and beat until creamy. Beat in the eggs. Mix in dry ingredients well. Stir in chocolate chips and nuts. Drop by teaspoons onto greased cookie sheets. Bake 8-10 minutes.

MARY WALKER

Bolinas author Mary Walker sat down, adjusted her glasses, and began her story in a lilting southern accent. It was a Sunday afternoon reading by local authors, part of the Spring Festival of Literary Arts. Walker's audience was caught spellbound in the cadence of her words; her story was a cliffhanger.

With Texas hospitality, at her home the next day, she poured tea in pretty china cups and served shortbread cookies as she spoke of the writing craft. "I've written screenplays, columns, children's and teens' books, and for newspapers. But I think the most difficult kind of writing is for children. Each word is so important. It's like poetry.

"Most American writers are taught to write short stories first. It's a very American form. Good ones are jewels, with no appendages; whereas a novel is a necklace, with episodes and digressions.

"Some people write religiously from 9 to 12 each day. Some folks sit in front of the typewriter until something comes to 'em. Days they'll sit, waiting. I don't do that. I don't sit down until I know what I'm going to do. But once I'm working, I'll work for 10 hours, if I can," she said.

Walker has published five "young adult" books, most recently *Brad's Box* (1988). Her first book, *Year of the Cafeteria* (1971), brought her the Dorothy Canfield Fisher Prize, was printed in paperback, and has been used in eighth-grade literature texts.

"You don't get rich, but they pay you," she said with a smile. "Have I lived on my writing? Oh, no, no no. As one playwright used to say, 'You can make a killing, but you can't make a living.' "

A creative writing teacher at the University of San Francisco and Dominican College, she offered this advice to new writers.

"You begin by writing," she said. "But one of the biggest obstacles is simply admitting you're a writer. To yourself and other people. It's hard to say, 'This is important to me.' You can get distracted by laundry, phone calls, lunches, visits from friends. Friends will often say, 'Gee, you can do that anytime.' But you can't. You could put it off for a lifetime. I advise using the answering machine."

She declined my invitation to talk about her work-in-progress. "It's too satisfying to talk about it. I think it loses energy that way, and you never get around to writing it. It's just too good an outlet."

Mary offers us this recipe for light and delicious cookies, entreating bakers to use only good, *Texas* pecans.

Texas Pecan Cookies

Ingredients:

1 egg white
1 cup light brown sugar
1-1/2 cups Texas pecan halves

Method:

Beat egg white in a bowl until stiff. Gradually beat in sugar until it becomes a creamy consistency. Add pecans. Drop by spoonful on a greased cookie sheet. Bake at 250 degrees for 30 minutes. These are like meringues, and will rise and turn golden brown. Remove from pan quickly.

CATHIE PONCIA

After 25 years of dairy farming, Al and Cathie Poncia of Tomales have reached the end of an era. They sold their dairy cows to a young couple, keeping only heifers and beef cattle, and said goodbye to a dairy business which has been in the family for 88 years. But while there may be nostalgia in leaving the business, there is also an unmistakable giddiness in the family. Is it utter relief and the lightness of new-found freedom?

For the first time in 17 years, none of their four children, Jennifer, Melissa, Jessica or Loren, are in grade school. "Shall I count the number of PTA meetings I've been to?" asked Cathie. While she's been supportive of her husband Al, she is glad to see his long days and grueling work come to an end.

To wit, Al came through the kitchen with a sparkle and bounce in his stride, full of talk about his training as a runner and mountain climber. He's climbed Mt. Whitney, expects to get to Half Dome in the summer, and has entered several foot races. As he put it, "I just want to see what's left in this ol' body before I hit 50."

"I had no idea what dairy life was about until I married Al," said Cathie. "What an eye opener. It's a tremendous commitment. It limits your family life. Al often came in after the kids were asleep. Exhausted, he'd ask, 'How was your day?' eat, and fall into bed."

A 4-H leader and 4-H camp nurse as her children were growing up, Cathie realized that being far out in the country, emergency response time was slow. If something happened to Al or the kids, she wanted to be prepared. So she took a class in Basic First Aid at Santa Rosa Junior College, and kept taking courses, entering the Emergency Medical Training School and becoming an attendant for the Bodega Bay Area Rescue, a volunteer ambulance company.

"I started out with no medical training at all — I was a housewife... but I fell in love with the work." Since then she's taught first aid and CPR in the Sonoma County area, for Petaluma Valley Hospital, Santa Rosa Memorial Hospital, the American Heart Association (Emergency Cardiac Care Program), the Farm Bureau and Bodega Bay's Fire Protection District, to name a few places.

A singing career has paralleled her work as a paramedic. "I started singing around the campfire with the 4-H kids. The camp cook and I'd play guitar and teach songs. That was Mike Tomasini, and we're still singing together. It mushroomed, and people asked us to sing for weddings, and parties and civic groups and even funerals. We sing ballads, folk songs and even soft rock," she said. "When I sing I get to share my voice and make others happy. When I teach, I can show people basic skills that can make all the difference in the survival of an injured or ill individual. I think these things have made me want to share even more. I'm proud to be a part of this community.

"When you put out a little of your time and yourself, you get back so much more," said Cathie, as she gave me this recipe, a delicious bit of decadence.

Black Bottom Cupcakes

Ingredients:

8 oz. cream cheese
1 unbeaten egg
1/3 c. sugar
1/4 tsp. salt
1- 6 oz. pkg. chocolate chips

1-1/2 cup flour
1/4 cup cocoa (unsweetened)
1/2 tsp. salt
1 cup sugar
1 tsp. baking soda

1 cup water
1/3 cooking oil
1 Tbsp. vinegar
1 tsp. vanilla

Method:

Combine and beat well: cream cheese, egg, 1/3 cup of sugar, and 1/4 tsp salt.
Stir in chocolate chips. Set aside.

Sift together: flour, cocoa, salt, 1 cup sugar and 1 tsp. baking soda.

In a mixing bowl add water, oil, vinegar and vanilla to the sifted ingredients.
Fill cupcake papers 1/2 full with chocolate batter. Top each with one heaping teaspoon of cream cheese mixture. Sprinkle top with sugar and chopped nuts. Bake at 350 degrees for 30-35 minutes.

DRINKS & WHATNOT

TERRY GARTHWAITE

The band, Joy of Cooking, has graced us with its upbeat rhythms and thoughtful lyrics for more than 20 years. The musicians have gone their separate ways, but on occasion they reunite. Terry Garthwaite, their lead instrumentalist and song writer, lives in San Geronimo.

Garthwaite's attention at the moment is focused on a project called Grounds for Art. Working with Barbara Stevenson, her goal is to create a stimulating, artistic program for both children and adults in the valley.

When her son, Sasha, became school-aged, she became concerned with the school arts programs. "As a parent, it irked me to have to pay extra for art and music in the schools. So we discussed the possibility of an arts center."

In a survey of Valley residents, it turned out that the community agreed. And they went one better. Since they also wanted a sports and recreation center, and many were willing to volunteer time to such programs, they created the umbrella organization, ARCC, Arts Recreation and Culture Complex.

Grounds For Art proposes a "Living Gallery," housed in the Valley, where there would be bi-monthly exhibits of artists' work, supported by lectures, workshops, classes for children and adults both during and after school. Springing from this "seed," would be a program of personal contact with professional artists and weekly visits by children to their studios in the area. It would

also include a program of art instruction for school children and teachers, a Van Go program, similar to the DeYoung Museum program which takes art shows, classes and workshops to other places.

Garthwaite patted a stack of paper and documents on her table. "This project is very interesting for me because it's about visual arts. I am basically a *sound* artist, but it's the same thing — the creative process. It's great to work with people from other perspectives... It regenerates ideas, stirs up the creative juices.

"Joy of Cooking is an opportunity to play in the band music I've loved, but my musical growth is going in a different direction." She reflected for a moment. "I was also happy working with the threesome of Sorrels, Hawkins and Garthwaite. We used to say we had the best seat in the house, because we held each other in high regard. Those women are fascinating, articulate, wise and a little weird.

"Happiness has been a theme in my music, but things I'm doing now are much more textural and tonally conscious. I am in a period of slowing down, evaluating, and working in solitude. I spend more time in my studio — just me and my 8-track."

A lover of Indian food, Garthwaite gives this recipe, adding "I'm not a fan of sugar, but it's very good." She also gives us a cookie recipe to go with your lassi.

Lassi Yogurt Drink

Ingredients:

1 cup unflavored yogurt
1 tsp. ground cumin
3-4 cups ice water
1/2 cup sugar
1 dash rosewater
1 pinch cayenne
1 pinch nutmeg

Method:

Combine yogurt and cumin in blender. Slowly pour thin stream of ice water. Add sugar, continue blending, add other ingredients. Serve immediately.

All Purpose Cookie Recipe

Ingredients:

1 cube butter or margarine
1/4 cup honey
2 cups flour
2 tsp. baking powder
2 tsp. vanilla
Optional: Carob, chocolate chips, raisins, nuts, sunflower seeds.

Method:

The beauty of this recipe is that you can throw everything together in a Cuisinart, in any order and it will come out well. Preheat oven to 350 degrees. When ingredients are mixed together to a smooth consistency, add optional items. Drop in spoonfuls on a greased cookie sheet. Bake for 10 minutes, until golden brown.

JEAN & PAUL BERENSMEIER

Most folks in the San Geronimo Valley area associate the name Jean Berensmeier with community activism. An advocate for the preservation of open space, Mrs. Berensmeier has been instrumental in land preservation as a County Parks and Recreation commissioner since the early 1960s. In 1973 she helped design the first community plan as part of the newly formed San Geronimo Planning Group. She's been on the San Geronimo Valley Cultural Center board since 1968.

What most folks don't know is that for 33 years, Berensmeier has also taught physical education at the College of San Mateo. Until her son, Paul, was born, she taught dance, directed performances, and coached the men's and women's fencing teams. She has instructed massage for 12 years, taught backpacking courses, bicycle camping, women's weight training, fitness and aerobics. As of this meeting, she still teaches four to five days a week.

"Paul [Berensmeier] is just completing his Master's in Sports Psychology," she said proudly. "Paul is a dicathlete." The dicathlon involves two days and 10 competitive events. It's the Olympic ideal of balanced body and mind — to run fast, jump high and throw hard. He was on his way out the door for a long run, up the fire trail to the ridge behind their home.

Land issues are foremost on Mrs. Berensmeier's mind these days. She said that in

1985, a survey showed that 40 percent of the people in the Valley were brand new. They didn't know or remember any of the battles for Barnabe Ridge or the Hendricks and Horne issue — battles which, for Berensmeier, were important victories in deterring development. "Nobody's lasted as long as I have in the battle to keep the land open space. The battle's never over... There's always the new guy that wants to put in a sewer system where there's never been a sewer system," she said, shaking her head.

It all started when she saw the 1961 masterplan for San Geronimo Valley, she explained. It was planned for 5,000 homes and 25,000 people. "When I found out, I said, 'That's not right. This valley is the most beautiful valley in the whole Bay Area.' For me, it's elemental. When you hear the birds sing or the creek babble, there's just no question. I helped to arrange for the state parks' purchase of the ridge for open space. Now a person can walk all the way from the valley to the ocean on undeveloped public lands. The salmon come up the creek to spawn in Woodacre — all the way to the middle of Marin. That's worth fighting for."

"Friends of mine say, 'But [they] can only build 26 houses [on the ridge].' And I say, 'But I don't want *one* house.' I'm going to the wall on this one. Retaining the rural character of this beautiful valley is absolutely critical to me."

Vanilla Yogurt Cheese

Ingredients:

1 16 or 32 oz. container of non-fat vanilla yogurt (or plain)
white paper towels or cheesecloth
Optional: Homemade blackberry jam, hot pepper jam or fresh herbs

Method:

Line a colander or strainer with two layers of paper towels. Place yogurt on paper towels. Cover with 2 paper towels. Place in refrigerator over a bowl for 8-10 hours for 16 oz. cheese, (11-13 hrs for 32 oz.). Dispose of paper toweling and place yogurt cheese in covered container. Makes about 1-1/2 cups. Keeps about four weeks.

Hints: Try also plain yogurt. Add herbs. A little salt. Great appetizer. Substitute for cream cheese in pies, appetizers and main dishes.

Spread on toast or muffins with homemade blackberry jam or as an appetizer with hot pepper jam over crackers.

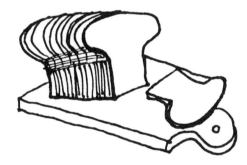

JACQUETTA NISBET

Pixieish and lively, renowned textile artist Jacquetta Nisbet of Inverness told the tale of her 35-year study of Native American traditions. She holds a deep reverence for the strength of spirit and artistry of the ancient civilizations of the Native American people — North, South and Central — with a particular interest in Peruvian (the most advanced weaving techniques found in the world) and Bolivian weavings.

In her studio, she set a magnifying glass down on the fibers of one old Peruvian weaving, explaining that these ancient people spun by hand threads "thinner than machines can now produce." I peeked in to view these hair's-breadth filaments which were twisted in twos, and woven into the intricately patterned cloth.

The mind balks to think how long this must have taken. I asked about the rate of progress on her intricate weavings-in-progress, on various looms (inkle, floor, and Navajo rug loom). "Oh, an inch a day on that lizard weaving there, and much faster, an inch an hour on this pattern," she said.

Jacquetta's determination and stamina became evident early on. At the age of five, she set off alone, to climb her first mountain. "Both my mother and father believed in the importance of physical training. We took enormously long hikes."

Jacquetta studied painting and sculpture at Edinborough College of Art in Scotland where she was trained in the discipline of a 12-hour day. In one of her art classes at the College, she met her partner and future husband, Nori.

But it wasn't until Nori and Jacquetta came to New York City that Jacquetta was introduced to weaving. "I went to an artists' cooperative and met Florence House of Columbia University, then in her 70s. I did illustrations in exchange for weaving lessons. The first thing I did was make my own loom. I was taught the principles right from the start. Then I found Native American weavings. The more I saw, the more deeply attracted I was. Nobody taught these weaves, so I had to figure out how they worked on my own. The next thing I knew, people asked would I teach them."

One recent summer, Jacquetta backpacked eight miles into Keet Seel, Arizona, to explore the ruins of the Anasazi culture. "One of the rangers shared my interest, and together we found plied cordage, potttery shards, and exchanged information." Then she added, thoughtfully, "It's odd that a Scot who grew up in a green, green climate would feel most at home in the pink, dryness of the desert, but I find tremendous peace and spiritual freedom there."

Here are two recipes from the Nisbets for runners, walkers and all kinds of nutritious breakfast eaters.

Killer Breakfast

Ingredients:

1 banana
1 cup orange juice
1 heaping Tbsp. ground almonds
1 heaping Tbsp. oat bran
1 heaping Tbsp. wheat germ
3-4 Tbsp. blueberry granola
fresh fruit

Method:

For each person, whip one banana til soft in bowl, add orange juice and mix. Pile on top ground almonds, oat bran, wheat germ, blueberry granola, and top with fresh fruit (strawberries, blueberries). It's delicious in layers or mix it up.

Killer Breakfast Two

Ingredients:

3 cups water
1 cup nine-grain breakfast cereal
1 banana
juice of one lemon
juice of one orange

Method:

Put water in a pot, heat until boiling, then add cereal, stir in, turn to low and go out on your run, up to one hour. Mash the banana, mixing well, and add juice of orange and lemon. Then mix in a cup or so of the cooked cereal. It is delicious without any sweetener, Jacquetta says, but added oat bran is nice.

JENNY GROAT

Artist Jenny Groat sat serenely in her two-story studio next to Lagunitas Creek. Outside, the trees filtered the afternoon sun, and opened to gardens where she and her husband, Piet, raise most of their own vegetables. A large cat rubbed past my calf. I was, years ago, a calligraphy student of hers; memories flooded back from that time.

Underspoken, as always, I gradually learned that she has become internationally known as a painter since that time, exhibiting and teaching throughout the US, Canada and Europe. Her paintings have been published in numerous books and periodicals. She has taught at College of Marin for 10 years.

I learned also that while she still does calligraphy, her current focus is painting. "I am returning with delight," she wrote, "to the full world of the fine arts."

Her first artistic career began as a piano major at the University of Pacific in Stockton. "I wasn't so good at piano, but I had an excellent creative dance teacher. After three years I literally ran away to San Francisco to dance," she said. That was the beginning of a 19-year career as a choreographer and dancer. She was Jenny Hunter, then. The company was called Dance West, on Clement Street.

But in 1968, at 38, Groat found herself unable to continue the dance. She explained, "It was a very painful time. I knew I needed another art form, but I didn't know what. I had no voice, no skill at anything. I camped out a lot, renewed my contact with Zen, nature and Jungian therapy, and went into retreat for five years."

As she emerged from this transitional time, Groat recalls, "Starting out with handwriting (calligraphy) seemed fairly innocuous. My husband supported me in so many ways. When we first talked of marriage, I said if he wanted a wife to stay home and cook, he'd better look elsewhere because I am an artist. He decided he liked it. He loves to cook. He is my best critic. He taught me how to think and verbalize about my artwork. He does everything he can to help me free my time. People sometimes comment on how lucky I am. But most male artists have a woman behind them. Why not be a woman with a man behind her?"

Now, Jenny Groat is producing abstract and figurative drawings and paintings in her spacious studio, combining the disciplines and studies of all of her earlier art years, music, theatre, dance and the visual arts.

Here is a delicious breakfast recipe which Jenny and Piet Groat enjoy after their morning meditation, before the day's work begins:

Piet and Jenny's Breakfast For Two

Ingredients:

1/2 tub soft tofu
6 oz. fruit nectar
8 oz. unflavored low-fat yogurt
1/2 tsp. vanilla
1 cup fresh fruit (strawberries, mango, papayas, kiwi, pineapple, banana)

Method:

Preparation is complex. Throw it all into a blender and blend on low speed until smooth. Pour into mugs or eat with a spoon like a cold soup. This is all you need until noon.

JIM FRIEDRICH

Jimmy Friedrich is in a pickle — business that is. I visited Friedrich at his "secret" garden on the Bolinas mesa where he grows "Bolinas Foods" pickles. It's a business which got started back in 1980 during a town meeting devoted to "How to Survive the 80s." Friedrich, Bob Scarola and Warren Weber signed up for the agricultural committee.

"The question for us," explained Friedrich, "was how to keep the produce here. So we started a cannery in town, and called it "Bolinas Foods." We went to Food Processing school, a four-day course at UC Davis, where you learn basic sterilization and canning techniques. We found out that high-acid fermented foods were exempt from health inspections and recall numbers; we decided to go with pickles."

Friedrich walked me down the irrigated rows of small cucumber plants. "This last crop isn't doing too well in this fog," he said. "I was counting on an Indian summer, which we didn't get. So the next crop will go in in April." He also grows potatoes, cabbage, beets, lettuce, peas, broccoli, spinach, chard, and 11 varieties of Jesse Schwartz's apple trees. The half-acre garden is protected from deer by an eight-foot, handmade eucalyptus fence.

"This is the dormant season," he continued. "Every piece of land needs to have a time to rest. If you keep messing with the land, you have to add a lot more to it. My philosophy about growing

things comes from Fukuoka's 'One Straw Revolution.' I named this One Straw Gardens. It's a Zen idea; To be an intuitive gardener, you can't take a course; you have to observe plants for 30 years. Then, you either have it or you don't." He grinned and shrugged, "This is mainly an educational hobby for me."

We ducked into a long plastic-covered hothouse, stuffed with tomatoes and peppers, perfumed by an occasional basil plant. "This is the first year of the hothouse," said Friedrich. "I got all greedy and put in too many tomatoes and couldn't keep up with them. Next year, I'll put in fewer and put the jalapenos on the west side."

Much of his all-organic produce is sold at the Bolinas People's Store, but the pickles are sold in health food stores all over the Bay Area. "Nobody makes a real pickle anymore. We do it the way they made them before the days of canning," he said, and launched into a story. "A visiting older gentleman took a bite of one of the pickles and tears came to his eyes. He said he hadn't tasted a real pickle in 30 years, and they'd called them 'sneak pickles' as a boy, because they stole 'em from the barrel."

These pickles aren't made with vinegar. They're soaked in a salt brine, fermented with spices and garlic, and packed in their own juice. The sugar in the cuke ferments to make its own vinegar. Friedrich says when he thumps the barrel and there are no bubbles, they're done. Here's a recipe to try.

Old Fashioned Sneak Pickles

Ingredients:

1 gallon water
10 lbs. pickling cucumbers
1/3-1/2 cup salt
garlic, chopped (at least 1 head)
dill weed
hot peppers
turmeric
cayenne (spice to taste)

Method:

In a ceramic or glass pot (not metal), cover cucumbers with salt water. Add garlic and spices. Cover loosely. It'll start bubbling in 2-3 days. Skim off bubbles occasionally, and keep the kids out of it. Ready in about three weeks. When you can thump the barrel or pot, and no bubbles come up, you're done, and the pickles are ready.

SUZANNE CONLEY

Slide Ranch is a year-round camp for all ages, located just off of Highway 1 north of Muir Woods. A slide has temporarily closed the road, and the absence of traffic made it blissfully quiet, as if one had stepped back in time. I ambled down the winding dirt road past a well-kept beehive overseen by a scarecrow and several charming, dilapidated buildings.

A small staff of three, along with four to five interns handle 5,000 to 6,000 visitors a year, instructing them in the art of respecting nature, five days a week. The only guideline for appropriate behavior, says Program Director Suzanne Conley, is to respect each other, the land and the animals. The 134-acre ranch has been in business for about 20 years now, giving similar programs.

The reflection of the afternoon sun off the ocean gave the whole ranch a luminous golden glow. Folks lounged in a hammock and in tall grass next to the gardens. A barefooted woman and child shared an artichoke on the picnic table on the deck of the office building. It was about as idyllic and peaceful a scene as you'll find.

Conley chuckled at my remarks to that effect, and informed me a group of 35 fourth-graders had departed only minutes before my arrival. "When they first come to the Ranch, they are rambunctious, giggling and full of it. But when they leave, after hiking down to the ocean a couple of times a day, sleeping and living outside, they are exhausted ... and calm," she said.

That is what Slide Ranch is all about — giving all ages the experience of living on a farm, taking care of animals and the land. It's hands-on work, like milking a goat, harvesting and planting a garden, and it's fun, like exploring the tidepools.

"We try to give them a body memory of what sheep's wool feels like and smells like, or what a wet egg that's just been laid looks like or the warmth of fresh goat milk," explained Suzanne. "We like to mix the scientific approach with the hands-on experience. We have programs for everyone from pre-schoolers to senior citizens. Our target is inner city or lower income people, ethnic groups and the disabled, who would not normally get such an experience."

Originally a Portuguese dairy farm, the ranch buildings are reconstructed buildings from the 1916 World Trade Fair which were dismantled, and brought to the ranch's site on the ocean. In the 1960s, the Nature Conservancy bought the land to prevent it from falling into the hands of developers. In 1975 the ranch became part of the newly forming Golden Gate National Recreation Area (GGNRA).

During the days of the Nature Conservancy, the caretaker, who loved children and animals, invited his children's classes out to spend time "back to nature." It was named the "Frontier Arts Institute" and taught what's being taught now.

Here's a recipe from Slide Ranch's Suzanne Conley.

Suzanne's Soft-Curd Farmer's Cheese

Ingredients:

1 gallon whole milk
1/4 cup vinegar
1 quart buttermilk
herbs and spices to taste

Method:

Heat milk to the point of boiling, but don't boil. (It won't curdle if you boil). Add buttermilk at room temperature and vinegar and spices. Let stand 15 minutes. Strain through cheesecloth or small wire mesh colander.

For a sweet cheese: Use coriander, a pinch of cinnamon, vanilla or fruit juice and small diced pieces of fruit such as peach or pear.

For a curry cheese: Use cumin, curry and tumeric (makes it turn yellow)

For fresh herb cheese: Use a pinch of rosemary, summer savory, marjoram, onion, chive, garlic and or fresh basil.

Sweet and Sour Whey Soup

Suzanne offers this recipe to make with the leftover whey from making the Farmer's Cheese. She says you can also make quick breads, like cornbread with the whey.

Ingredients:

For one gallon of whey stock:
1/4 cup tamari
1/4 cup honey
1 clove garlic
1/8 cup rice vinegar (if whey is not very sour
 already)

Add:
2 cubes tofu
3 grated carrots
1 chopped onion
oil for sauteeing
2 cups greens, such as spinach or swiss chard

Method:

Whey stock:
Strain the whey a second time, as it will continue to curdle. Then add tamari, honey, garlic and rice vinegar, if needed.

Add:
Sauté in frying pan until carrots and onions are softened, at last minute add 2 cups of greens. Add vegetables to whey stock.

FOUR PUMPKIN PIES

The season of ghouls and goblins is the time to carve, cook, illuminate, hold, smash, mash, taste and otherwise enjoy the stately pumpkin. These giant squashes seem to hide, sheltered under big green leaves, until well into fall. Then one day the leaves suddenly fall away to reveal bright orange spheres. Here are the best of the pumpkin pie recipes:

Maple Pumpkin Chiffon

Submitted by Cathay Loadman, this pie is light and fluffy, a relief if you've overeaten the main course. Make it in a pre-cooked pie shell (or graham cracker crust).

Ingredients:

1 4-5 lb. pumpkin or winter squash
1/2 cup milk
1 Tbsp. gelatin in 1/4 cup cold water
1/2 cup maple syrup
3 egg yolks, beaten slightly (set aside whites)
1/2 tsp. ginger, cinnamon, nutmeg
1/4 tsp. allspice

Method:

Cook all ingredients, except gelatin and 1/4 c. of syrup, over double boiler until thick. Add gelatin, stirring until dissolved. Cool these ingredients. Whip 3 eggs whites until stiff. When pumpkin mixture begins to set, stir in 1/4 c. additional syrup. Fold in egg whites. Fill pie shell. Chill pie for several hours. Serve w/ whipped cream.

Fresh Pumpkin & Coconut

Submitted by writer Margo Patterson Doss, of Bolinas from her years living in Samoa. "Shortages are part of living on an island. If the boat or plane doesn't come, the cook may have to 'make do.' Thus the fresh pumpkin and coconut pie, which Samoan cooks put together if there are no eggs on the island."

Ingredients:

Crust:
1 cup whole wheat pastry flour
1 stick butter or marg.
1/4-1/2 cup honey
1 cup toasted coconut
water, if necessary
Filling:
1 small pumpkin, cut up
1/2 stick butter/marg.
1/2 cup coconut milk, canned
1/2 cup honey
1 Tbsp. molasses
1/4 tsp. cinnamon
1/8 tsp. nutmeg, cloves, allspice
1" fresh ginger

Method:

Mix crust ingredients. Press into 9" pie pan. Steam pumpkin with ginger. Cook, remove skin. Drain, mash. Add coconut milk to pumpkin and mix well. Pour into pie shell. Bake at 400 degrees for 15 to 20 minutes. Top with toasted coconut or coconut cream.

Pumpkin Peanut Butter

This is an old Baltimore recipe from Emily Childs, who's mother operated the first hotel for blacks in Baltimore. Preheat oven to 425 degrees.

Ingredients:

Rich crust:
1-1/2 cup unbleached flour
10 Tbsp. (1-1/4 sticks) chilled unsalted butter
5 Tbsp. well chilled solid vegetable shortening
6 Tbsp. ice water

Filling:
1- 16 oz. can packed pumpkin
2 tsp. vanilla
3/4 cup firmly packed light
   brown sugar
3 eggs
1/2 cup creamy peanut butter
1-1/4 cup half & half
1/4 cup Drambuie or
   other cordial
1/2 tsp. grated nutmeg

Method:

Cut shortening and butter into small bits. Mix flour, butter and shortening until consistency of coarse meal. Add 1 tablespoon of water at a time until dough comes together. Gather, refrig. 30 minutes Roll out 1/8" thick.

Mix sugar, pumpkin and peanut butter in large bowl. Blend in eggs, one at a time. Stir in half & half, liqueur, vanilla, nutmeg, salt to taste. Pour into prepared shell. Bake 20 min. Reduce heat to 350. Continue baking until filling is set. (50 min) Cool on rack. It'll fall in the center.

Edith Mitchell's Pumpkin Pie

Dave Mitchell's (editor of *The Pt. Reyes Light*) mother always made two of these pies at a time, since her 14-year-old son Dave would consume one whole pie before they completely cooled. He says, "It's an incredibly good pumpkin pie. Once I tasted this, I couldn't believe anybody ate any other kind."

Ingredients:

1 large can pumpkin
2 Tbsp. molasses
1 cup each white and brown sugar
1/4 tsp. each ginger, cloves
3 tsp. cinnamon
4 eggs, slightly beaten
2 cups scalded milk

Method:

Beat eggs. Add above ingredients, hot milk last. Put in two 9" unbaked pie crusts. Bake at 425 degrees for 45 minutes.

A Swedish Christmas

A little before Christmas in Sweden, on Dec. 13 to be exact, there is a celebration called Santa Lucia day. It is a celebration of light, at the darkest time of the year, as well as a remembrance of Saint Lucia, the queen of light.

Legend has it that she traveled by foot and by ship with her disciples, around Sicily and the Mediterranean, giving food to the poor. One version of the story tells of her landing on an island where the people were starving. Her ship was stocked for a long voyage, but upon landing, she gave it to the islanders in need. The Portuguese people also adopted her as a saint, and no one knows exactly how she was transported to Sweden, but these were seafaring nations, the world's best navigators.

Swedish children traditionally rise before light on this day (the sun doesn't come up until 9 or 10 a.m. in Sweden) before their parents, go to the kitchen and prepare coffee, Lucia buns, and gingerbread to bring up to their parent's bedroom. I didn't ask who cleans up the kitchen later.

Halley Sanders, a first grader at the time of this photograph in the Bolinas-Stinson School models her Santa Luca crown, which she made while studying "Winter Holidays Around the World" in Jane Gregory's classroom.

At the Santa Lucia festival this year in San Francisco, Lucia emerged in a long, white lace gown, with red sash. A wreath of lingonberry branches and crown of lighted candles created a halo, as she walked and sang, followed by a train of blonde girls, also dressed in white, holding candles. "I cried. I always cry. It's so nostalgic a time for me," said Swedish-born Eva Lindholm of Bolinas, as she described the festival.

Eva gave us the Swedish Christmas recipe for Risgrynsgrot, which is a rich rice pudding. It is thick, sweet and delicious. Into the pudding, traditionally goes just one almond. Whoever gets the almond gets either his or her wish, or gets married next. Also, says Eva, one must say a rhyme before eating the porridge. Usually it's a funny rhyme about being gluttonous.

West Marin artist and transplanted Swede Karin Wikstrom described a kind of candy children love at Christmas, called Knack (pronounced Knock with a hard K). It's made in little paper cups, and it's dense and sticky; one of the filling-loosener kind. You pop the whole think in your mouth and retrieve the paper later.

Recalling her Swedish childhood, Ulla McLean of Point Reyes Station described the Christmas season begining on Lucia Day. "From then until New Years, the hustle and bustel begins with lots of homebaked goodies and specialty foods such as her favorite Frestelse, a creamy potato dish.

Here are the recipes these three Swedes have described.

Risgrynsgrot

Ingredients:

1 cup rice
2 cups water
2 cups milk
3 mandarin oranges, peeled
1 cinnamon stick
1/4 cup maple syrup
1-1/2 pints whipping cream
1 almond

Method:

Cook rice in water with cinnamon stick until done. Add milk, stir, cook again for a while until thick. Add syrup. Refrigerate until chilled. Whip the cream until stiff. Fold into porridge. Stir in mandarin orange slices and cinnamon. Enjoy while hoping you get the almond.

Knack

Ingredients:

3/4 cup heavy whipping cream
3/4 cup golden syrup
1/3 cup finely chopped almonds
1/4 cup sugar
Optional: 4 Tbsp. breadcrumbs
1/4 tsp. baking soda

Method:

Mix cream, syrup and sugar in a thick-bottomed pot. Boil until it gets sticky (125 degrees C.) for about 25 minutes, stirring occasionally. Test to see if it is at the soft ball stage by dropping a bit in cold water. When it has reached this stage, add almonds and optional ingredients. Pour into a pouring pitcher and then into tiny paper cups.
Note: the breadcrumbs extend the recipe a little. The baking soda makes the candy more pourous.

Janson's Frestelse

Ingredients:

6 medium potatoes
1 can anchovy-style sprats
3/4 cup cream
2 medium onions, chopped
3 Tbsp. butter
salt and pepper

Method:

Cut potatoes into fine spears. Put half of them in bottom of a greased casserole dish. Sauté onions and add a layer on top of potatoes. Spread anchovy sprats evenly, add rest of onions and finish with potatoes. Place butter on top, and sprinkle with salt and pepper. Pour cream over all. Place in 350 degree oven for 45-60 minutes until potatoes are browned.

INDEX BY RECIPE

INDEX BY RECIPE

INDEX BY RECIPE

INDEX BY COOK

INDEX BY COOK